SANTA FE
HOUSES

SANTA FE HOUSES

CHRISTINE MATHER
SHARON WOODS

PHOTOGRAPHS BY JACK PARSONS

CLARKSON POTTER/PUBLISHERS
NEW YORK

Published by Clarkson Potter/Publishers, New York, New York. Member of the Crown Publishing Group,
a division of Random House, Inc.
www.randomhouse.com

CLARKSON N. POTTER is a trademark and POTTER and colophon are registered trademarks of Random House, Inc.

Printed in China

Design by Donna Agajanian

Library of Congress Cataloging-in-Publication Data is available upon request.

ISBN 0-609-60647-6

10 9 8 7 6 5 4 3 2 1

First Edition

ACKNOWLEDGMENTS

We are in awe—and sometimes a bit envious—of the creative spirits, kind souls, and generous individuals who have received us with affection into their homes. Sincere thanks to Doug Atwill, who is simply the best and gave inspiration to Billy Halsted and Wayne Bladh, and Joy and Bernie Busch, among others. Charmay Allred, Sandy and the late Diane Besser, Bud and Barbara Hoover, Tukey Koffen, Paul Pletka and Nancy Benkof are fellow folk art aficionados who share so many of my passions. Among those that raised the envy quotient to new levels are Ramona Scholder, Bill Schenck, Elizabeth Thorton, Jane and Tom O'Toole, Jane and John Bagwell, and Margery Hansen. Exquisite small homes are those of Joan Baker and S. Lyn and Doug Rose, while big-is-beautiful homes (often harder to do successfully) belong to Mr. and Mrs. Ron Dubin, Sandy and Russ Osterman, and Karen Berlanti. Bringing art to the indoors and out were Jody Apple, Sally Chandler and Ron Blankenship, Clare Rhodes and Richard Hughes, and Josette de la Harpe. Malcolm and Linda Alexander, Vincent and Anne Carrozza, and Ann and Kelly Shannon shared their homes and certainly make my neighborhood a great place to be. Artistic personalities with homes to match belong to Linda Durham, Luis Tapia and Carmella Padilla, Ashley and Paul Margetson, and Alice Ann Biggerstaff. Graceful and elegant abodes were created by Julio and June Davila, Gil and Eileen Hitchcock, Holly Logan and Bob Weinberg, and Dr. and Mrs. David Snyder. Omer and Bunny Claiborne, Bob and Pat Eggers, Richard and Nedra Matteucci, and Bill and Sam Field are generous friends and lovely folks with houses to match. Judy Dillenberg of The Clay Angel and Theo Raven of Doodlet's are two of Santa Fe's treasured ladies with outstanding homes. At the top of their professions are Pam Duncan, Jane Smith, John Midyette, Doug McDowell, and Michael Mahaffey—their homes display not only skill but heart. La Quinta Cultural Center and Los Poblanos Inn remind us of the rewards provided to us all by those dedicated to the preservation of our regional architecture.

The division of labor for this book involved myself as the writer, as well as what might be termed a project director, while Sharon, coordinating the scouting, scheduling, and directory, brought business sense to what we were doing, and helped keep the vision intact. We both looked through the lens, teased Jack endlessly, wrestled with the giant number of slides he produced, and had a great time together. At her office, Katie Delaney and Avenelle Gonzalez provided us with excellent support. Other folks here on the home front who helped out were John and Linda Dressman of the Flower Market and Jan Moss and David Margolis. A few thousand of miles away, in New York, we were blessed with an entire crew of thoughtful and kind folks who worked very hard in the production of this book. *Mil gracias* to Deborah Geltman and Gayle Benderoff, agents and trusted advisors. *Abrazos* to Annetta Hanna, my new editor, and Lauren Shakely, my old; they do what all great editors do—make you look good. *Felicitaciones* to our designer, Donna Agajanian, who shares this skill as well. Liz Royles helped in a hundred hidden ways, as did many others at Potter.

Finally, as the leader of this enterprise—the so-called head enchilada—I would like to thank Sharon Woods for her enthusiasm, energy, and judgment, and Jack Parsons, whose beautiful photography has elevated all of our efforts, giving us great pride in the outcome of our labor. *Salud*, love, and thanks to my husband, Davis; it was largely through his prodding that this project got under way and thanks to his support that it came to fruition.

Christine Mather
Santa Fe, New Mexico

CONTENTS

From a patio perched on a ridge, one can see clouds massing behind the Sangre de Cristo Mountains.

INTRODUCTION

That there is such thing as a "Santa Fe home" is a remarkable story. It's true that Santa Feans' homes share many things with houses throughout the world. They are places of comfort, family, protection, and status—but they are also homes born of a unique little community that holds a special place in the history of our country. Santa Fe's past cannot be separated from the fact that today the city's residents live in some of the most distinctive dwellings in our land. This, then, is not a book about architecture, or even design, but truly one of lifestyle and all that may imply. As "natives" or newcomers, we Santa Feans share in a style of living that is closely associated with our homes, reflecting the personality of our town, its history, and the natural world outside our doors.

Santa Feans are by nature self-deprecating, filled with ambivalence about the wonders of their town. We struggle with feelings of being trapped in a mythology created not just from the past, but also from a deep need to belong to someplace special. So while we recognize that our town may be, in part, the product of nostalgia, we certainly wouldn't want it to be just like everywhere else. We may be weary of hearing the virtues of adobe architecture extolled, but we cannot imagine living in a town of brick or wooden siding. We speak of our city as being "charmed out," but we cannot ignore the allure of water rushing down the acequia or the powerful sense of well-being experienced with one whiff of burning piñon. While we are "the city different," we are also "the city difficult"; this complexity, too, is part of our lives.

The self-effacing nature of the town is balanced by not just a little swagger. We Santa Feans revel in the attention we draw. We are "house-proud"; we expend

A detail of Santa Fe in the spring, with poppies against a white picket fence. A classic Santa Fe adobe home is in the background.

too much time and energy on our homes; we are over-invested in them in many ways. But we shrug and sigh with this self-knowledge, unable to give up what is so important a part of our identity. The fact that we admire and enjoy this wonderful vernacular architecture, are deeply invested in collecting things from our region, are creatively involved in the design of our interiors, and derive great pleasure from seeing one another's homes brings us directly into contact with the artistic process. Our lifestyle can be artful—sometimes touching and beautiful, though not perfect, not without vanities and foibles—but at least open to the possibility of art. In striving to bring creativity directly into our homes, we spend inordinate amounts of time staring at paint chips and wall surfaces, gazing at tiles and stucco samples, tracking down wizards of plaster and master fireplace builders. This is not true for all of us, of course, but a disproportionate number of folks here are deeply involved in the pursuit of a beautiful home. The proof lies in the recognition that for a relatively little town, there are hundreds of homes that are works of art—creative, personal, exciting, even provocative—and thousands of little visual delights in every corner of the city. So much of this derives from the place itself—the qualities of the climate, the physical setting—and from the strict, almost austere parameters of life that existed in the past.

Unspoken and often narrow expectations for homes in Santa Fe govern much of our lives here. While historic ordinances give rules for building in various areas of the town, there are countless covenants, both written and unwritten, that give us a structure in which we work. Those who come to Santa Fe for the first time are often struck by the town's uniform appearance. Critics find that our insistence upon visual consistency results in self-serving mythmaking. But art and creation are always dependent upon the efforts of those who came before. The references that Santa Feans make to bygone styles of living are reverential. By acknowledging that many people—Native Americans, Hispanic colonists, Iberian builders, Arabic inventors, Irish immigrants, German craftsmen, New World scholars, archaeologists, artists, and architects—have cast their influence upon the homes here, Santa Feans reveal their respect for the anonymous, the vernacular, the humble, the worker, and the housewife. Santa Fe has chosen to revere its past. We celebrate the good life that is possible here, and we claim that contributing to it can add immeasurably to the pleasures of being alive. All of this is done within the context of our most personally revealing possessions: our homes.

OPPOSITE: The sculptural nature of adobe is revealed in this entryway. ABOVE: The Prada home on Canyon Road has brick coping and wood-trimmed windows, details first added to homes during the Territorial Period (1846–1912) of New Mexico's history.

EARTH

Filled with the earthy hues of brown adobe and the brightness
of our snowy days, the season is winter, when the earth sleeps. We are
home-dwelling, borrowing from the Pueblos a timeless sense of place.

The distinctive lines and soft swellings of Santa Fe's adobe buildings come from the very nature of the material—plain, solid, heavy, malleable earth. Besides being of the earth, our homes are also earthy, that is, free from the elegance that comes with more refined materials. Much of this simplicity is directly related to patterns set by New Mexico's original inhabitants. Pueblo architecture, with its reliance upon available materials, hand-building, and interconnected structures, has been the model for our homes, as ancient ruins and timeless villages establish an unspoken standard for the region.

The prehistoric past of New Mexico is our mystery, a presence full of hints about the lives of the early people who lived here before us. The past is palpable everywhere. Geologically, it rings the state with mountains, sleeping volcanoes, and stratified layers of earth and bone that reveal the long passages of time. Perched on thick layers of volcanic ash turned to rock, there are long-abandoned villages strewn with pottery shards—evidence of vanished lives, duly recorded in the region's thousands of archaeological sites. Almost anywhere you now find water—as well as places where water once existed—you will find prehistoric human traces. The nature of the people who once lived here seems graceful, diligent, and complex, suggested by exquisite Clovis points, Mimbres pottery with its humorous images, and astounding Chaco Canyon, an archaeological site of great magnitude and mystery. Present-day New Mexico appears to be at the epicenter of a classical past with few parallels in the United States. The blending of this original culture with Spanish construction techniques and materials gave us architecture amenable to change but rooted in four hundred years of life.

Taos Pueblo in winter. The
most intact of the Eight
Northern Pueblos, this
multileveled structure serves as
a touchstone for all of the
regional architecture.

WINTER

Santa Fe is a winter place. It loves summer, adores fall, craves spring—but, like it or not, it is a winter place. In part, this is because winter can come at any time of the year, with hailstorms and snow arriving as late as April or as early as July. This gives an edgy quality to the other seasons, so when winter comes, it is a relief: We can totally engage with the cold and snow. Our homes are winter homes, thick and protected, well heated by numerous fireplaces. Just over our shoulders, the blanketed mountains reassure us that there will be water enough for the rest of the year, stored in their generous rivers of frozen snow. Our most intense celebrations take place over the winter months, with dances in the Pueblos and a long cycle of Christmas festivities. Decorated with lights or quietly suspended in time with a fresh layer of snow, the Plaza on Christmas Eve seems to welcome the entire town as people walk the streets of ancient neighborhoods to see the rows of *farolitos*—small lanterns created by setting votive candles in sand inside simple paper bags—sing carols, and join in the holy night's offerings.

ABOVE: A ladder to the night sky. OPPOSITE, TOP LEFT: Melting snow leaving the flat-roofed adobe home via a canal, or rainspout, has frozen. OPPOSITE, BOTTOM LEFT: A bell tower on a New Mexican adobe church. OPPOSITE, RIGHT: Moonrise over the Sangre de Cristo Mountains in winter.

Make an Entrance

New Mexico was a fortress society for hundreds of years. Homes and villages were built not just for shelter but for protection. Walls and gates, hidden entryways, small protected courtyards, narrow passageways, all could serve to block unwanted intruders. Larger, more formal gates were built to safeguard a passageway to a courtyard beyond, but today's gates continue to provide a first line of defense for the private lives of many Santa Feans.

ABOVE: These handsome antique doors serve as the gateway to the home beyond. Like entryways throughout the Latin world, they conceal much of what lies behind them and suggest that casual entry is discouraged. OPPOSITE, LEFT: Narrow double doors are fitted snugly into an adobe wall with an arch above. OPPOSITE, RIGHT: Not all entry gates are imposing, and some even provide a glimpse inside. These examples, with their well-weathered surfaces, seem quite approachable.

Doors

The classic approach to a Santa Fe home is through a door, which, though formidable, gives hints to what lies beyond. These doors speak of long history, of times when protection was vitally important and when homes were built with great care and physical labor. They are as individual as their owners. Painted doors are common, as well as doors with applied wooden designs. The earliest New Mexican homes often had openings rather than true doors, but once milled lumber was available there was an explosion of decorative options. Many of these designs still inspire carpenters today.

ABOVE: Classic Santa Fe doors with expansive glass and home-designed screens. RIGHT: Designed by architect and homeowner Michael Mahaffey, these large doors are decorated with hundreds of little *milagros*— small metal religious figures. OPPOSITE: A gorgeous hand-carved door and lintel were crafted in 1921 by the Santa Fe artist B.J.O. Nordfeldt.

Passageways

Santa Fe homes have unique entryways. Some of them are grand and explicit in keeping with the town's royal pedigree. Big double doors will open onto long wide hallways that lead directly into the home. Almost as if in deliberate contrast but just as typical, and perhaps more common, are small houses with so many entries that the visitor can end up baffled.

OPPOSITE: A broad entryway set with fine Navajo rugs. ABOVE LEFT: A lowered ceiling and beams and plaster carve out a little entryway to an old adobe home, allowing space to hang a hat and transition to the big room beyond. ABOVE: Old double doors lead to another hallway distinguished by a fine chest placed beneath a skylight. LEFT: A beautiful, wide entryway with a formidable wooden attack pig by Felipe Archuleta.

The *Sala*

Santa Fe's formal entries prepare the visitor for what is to follow, the grand *sala*, defined by its massive beams, elegant corbels, thick walls, wooden ceilings, and deep windows. These rooms should not be confused with living rooms, since they rarely invite any sort of casual lifestyle. Instead, *salas* and the entry-ways leading to them are impressive spaces meant to be gathering spots for large groups. Evocative of the stark naves of New Mexico's churches, they reveal the somber dignity and courtliness of aristocratic Spanish life. Few homes, of course, contain this type of room, reserved as it was for the wealthy and for ecclesiastical, government, or official buildings. Far more typical are small, simple living areas where everything is brought down to scale, although they may have elegant wooden ceilings similar to those of the *salas*. These intimate rooms and their hidden entryways provide all the comfort needed and offer far more in the way of security and warmth than most interiors of this size. As if cupped into the hollowed-out hand of the home, these safe spaces of modest dignity are the perfect places to be on a winter's night.

OPPOSITE: Deep windows pierce this high-ceilinged living area. ABOVE: Cool white walls and a big open room provide a setting for a fine collection of Native American and Spanish colonial art. The arched doorway reinforces the colonial ambiance of the room.

OPPOSITE: The living room of a photographer and world traveler reflects her interest in Asian art, which combines well with its new Santa Fe setting. ABOVE: This large formal living room is shared by two guest suites in an elegant guest house.

ABOVE: Skylights cut between the beams provide plenty of light for viewing collections. OPPOSITE, TOP: A large, light, spacious living room with high ceilings is far from formal, but rather a relaxed space. OPPOSITE, BOTTOM: A classic *sala* with a large central fireplace. The perfect proportions of this room are very much dictated by the span of the *vigas*, the dark surfaces of which are echoed in the beautiful antiques.

Ceilings, Beams, and Corbels

Besides the use of adobe, nothing has brought more distinction to the homes of Santa Fe than the tradition of using timbered ceilings. Time was when massive logs were harvested from the nearby mountains and carried into town on the backs of rugged little burros. Stripped of their bark and adzed into uniform pieces, these beams, or *vigas*, were laid at uniform intervals across the top of the adobe walls. Above them were placed either small peeled poles (*latillas*) or split planking (*rajas*). Topping this support would be a layer of dried vegetation and finally a substantial load of dirt. The more important the building, the more elaborate the ceiling, resulting in gorgeous and ingenious constructions of beautifully decorated wooden elements, especially in our churches. In these, corbels and other supporting elements such as moldings all contribute to lift the eye and the spirit heavenward, much as the flying buttresses and vaulted ceilings of European cathedrals do.

Adobe buildings could be only as wide as the beams available or affordable to their owners, so modest dwellings had small rooms. Perhaps this limitation, above all others, has led to the classic proportions that are the hallmarks of all fine adobe dwellings. Interestingly enough, even when milled lumber became available, the use of simple *vigas* and *latillas* continued; the relative poverty of the region enriched the architecture.

OPPOSITE: In a ceiling of surpassing beauty, the pieces that span the *vigas* are of split cedar, a wood that ages to a rich reddish hue. The unusual zigzag element makes for a lively and intricate design. ABOVE: The space between the *vigas* of this ceiling has been plastered into a graceful undulating pattern. LEFT: Small branches form the *latillas* that are placed between the *vigas*.

TOP: Two examples of distinctive wooden lintels. CENTER: Hand-carved and adzed surfaces with decorative detail. The ancient corbel was salvaged from an eighteenth-century structure. RIGHT: The door and window lintels were decorated by the artist B.J.O. Nordfeldt.

BELOW: Two beautifully hewn corbels not only serve as wonderful decorative details but also help distribute the weight of the roofs. RIGHT: Contemporary corbels are available at most of the lumberyards in town and are a common feature in almost all Santa Fe homes. BELOW RIGHT: Here, a notched log serves as both corbel and post for an old farm building.

Woodworking

The woodworker, the maker of furniture and cabinetry, the man of adz, awl, and plane is the unsung hero of Santa Fe. From slabs of plain pine he gave us surfaces to be notched, carved, and gouged. A vast repertoire of Native American, Spanish, and Arabic designs provided him with many decorative possibilities. Yet, few surfaces are overly elaborate; rather, the repertoire is so chastely used that the wood is allowed to show its virtues as a thing of organic and mutable beauty. Individual pieces take on a monastic or medieval simplicity. One aspect of woodworking dear to New Mexico is the use of adz marks to create surfaces rich in the details of handwork. Upon this rustic surface simple designs of regional choice—rosettes, shells, bullet notches, pomegranates—were carved, giving each cabinet, chair back, door, or cupboard a distinctive look related to some faraway place but so clearly of this area.

A pair of cabinet doors carved in the 1940s in a home designed by John Gaw Meem. Meem made great use of the design repertoire represented among the old pieces of New Mexican furniture he saw. The central rosette was one such popular design in colonial times, as was the meandering floral and pomegranate motifs. This type of shallow, elegant carving appeared on the early six-board chests that were important household items for colonists.

LEFT AND ABOVE: Two examples of built-in cupboards, using plain pine and few decorative details. OPPOSITE LEFT: The surface of this hand-hewn door clearly shows the adz marks of the carpenter. OPPOSITE, TOP RIGHT: A detail of a much more elaborate cupboard, probably Spanish. OPPOSITE, BOTTOM RIGHT: These paneled doors are the perfect backdrop for a fine old sombrero.

The Art of the Adobe Home

THE MEETING OF TWO HIGHLY
CREATIVE MINDS—THOSE OF
JOHN BRINCKERHOFF JACKSON
AND BILL SCHENCK—IS
REVEALED IN THIS LARGE ADOBE
HOME TO THE SOUTH OF SANTA
FE. JACKSON, A LANDSCAPE
ARCHITECT, BUILT THE HOUSE,
WHICH IS SOLIDLY NESTLED INTO
THE LANDSCAPE YET STILL
LINKED TO THE RURAL
COMMUNITY THAT GREW UP
AROUND THE WETLAND AREA
NEARBY. SCHENCK, AN ARTIST,
TOOK ON THE HOUSE WHERE
JACKSON HAD LEFT IT. ITS THICK
WALLS NOW SERVE AS A
GALLERY FOR SCHENCK'S
IMPRESSIVE COLLECTION OF
REGIONAL ART.

OPPOSITE: Each room has a fireplace. This one, with side *bancos*, displays a collection of Southwestern pottery on its mantel. Hanging above is a painting by Victor Higgins, part of a collection of regional art. LEFT: The study offers more glimpses of Schenck's collection of pottery and paintings. BELOW, LEFT AND RIGHT: He also owns an important collection of the furniture of Thomas Molesworth, an early twentieth-century Rocky Mountain furniture maker whose work once filled the cabin hideaways of the rich and famous.

RIGHT: Deep walls, a plastered dado, and the curve of the arch frame a view from the front hallway. BELOW: A detail of a stepped mantelpiece that offers more space for Schenck's collection. OPPOSITE LEFT: A roaring fire behind a silhouette fire screen. Above the fireplace, a painting by Victor Higgins. OPPOSITE RIGHT: A small desk by Molesworth, with its chair. They rest below some of the collection of prehistoric pottery, which is displayed on a cowboy-style shelf.

Nichos

There is something of such ancient rightness about the *nicho*, or niche. It has its universal origins in buildings of rock and earth, where a simple scooping-out yields a practical little space. And this is the beauty of adobe. Imagine that you would like a place to put your favorite Pueblo pot. You can dig a hole in your wall and fashion it into a cozy little shape with a flat bottom and an arched top that mimic the gentle curves of your pot. Like its outward cousin the *banco*, or bench, the *nicho* relies upon the delicious sculptural nature of adobe and plaster for its existence. Even in frame-and-stucco Santa Fe homes, the *nicho* remains an important decorative element, as if there is something missing if you can't find just the right spot *in* the wall— not *on* the wall.

Variations on the theme of *nichos*, each created for a special object. One *nicho* goes right through the wall so that it is visible from two separate areas. *Nichos* need not be made of adobe or plaster, as demonstrated by a wooden *nicho* set into a wall.

Old Santa Fe

BEHIND A GATE, BEYOND THE BUSTLE, ON A LITTLE DEAD-END STREET, SITS A QUINTESSENTIAL SANTA FE HOUSE BLESSED WITH ALL THAT SUCH A HOME HAS TO OFFER. LIKE MANY SUCH PERFECT OLD ADOBE HOMES, IT SURVIVED NEGLECT AND DECLINE. RENEWAL CAME WHEN S. LYN ROSE, AN INTERIOR DESIGNER, SAW THROUGH ITS DARKENED MESS TO THE BASIC BEAUTY BENEATH. ALONG WITH A THOROUGH RENOVATION, SHE ALSO ADDED FINE ETHNOGRAPHIC ANTIQUES. HER PASSION FOR GARDENING ENSURES THAT, WINTER OR SUMMER, THE HOUSE SITS LIKE A LITTLE GEM HIDDEN FROM VIEW BEHIND A WEALTH OF PLANTINGS AND SHELTERING ADOBE WALLS.

OPPOSITE, TOP: The home in winter after a fresh snow reveals its basic outlines of protruding *vigas,* with blue trim against the brown walls.

OPPOSITE, BOTTOM: Old doors, a wrought-iron grill, and a double corbel used as a fireplace mantel add special touches to the home. BELOW: The bedroom contains some of the ethnographic art that Rose collects.

ABOVE: Just as in a New Mexican church with its transverse clerestories, this living and dining area is bathed in light from above. OPPOSITE, LEFT: A small kitchen has all the basics, including a window with a view through the front porch, or portal. A simple rack provides extra storage space. OPPOSITE, RIGHT: Upright wooden beams and a dropped ceiling area carve out a separate space for an entryway and a display area for ethnographic pottery from Latin America.

ABOVE: An arched doorway leads from the dining and entry rooms to a sitting room beyond. Plain walls and a big mirror reflect light from the clerestory. OPPOSITE: Off the sitting area, a small space with big windows is used for writing and reading.

Books, Shelves, and Built-ins

The curse and the joy of the reader and the writer: books—stacks and stacks of them. In a town full of readers, writers, scholars, and collectors, books tend to multiply alarmingly. Santa Fe's wealth of regional scholarship is reflected in wonderful collections focusing on the people of the Southwest: Few Santa Feans can resist the pleasures of book collecting. But this hobby is also prevalent in a town notoriously short on storage spaces. What to do? Turn an extra doorway into a bookshelf; carve a giant niche into the wall to create a bookshelf; build shelves in; build them up; and finally, head to the used bookstore from time to time to unload a pile. Throughout the year, libraries, colleges, churches, and museums try to help us relinquish some of our books in massive sales, but it seems we buy back as many as we give up.

Besides books, our homes display collections of all types. This means that books must vie with collectibles for the available shelf and closet space. And of course, if you are a serious collector, you need books about your chosen area of collecting. Here's the riddle of the Santa Fe home: Which came first—the books or the collection?

OPPOSITE: A wonderful collection sits bedside in a home filled with English and Continental antiques. In this case, the space may once have been a window that was filled in when an early addition was made to the house, allowing for a great built-in space with a beautifully carved lintel. LEFT: Art books fill every available bit of space in this ingenious set of shelves surrounding an impressive carved door.

ABOVE: An elegant formal library with a bookcase built directly into the wall. RIGHT: The thick adobe walls of this home—revealed by the deeply set windows—allowed for bookcases and cupboards, turning a small passageway room into a useful reading area. Here, both books and collections share the shelf space.

Traditional Adobe

THE CLASSIC PROPORTIONS OF THIS GRAND OLD HOME CONFER UPON IT A SENSE
OF ARCHITECTURAL GRACE. IT IS EVIDENCE OF THE FINEST IMPULSES OF THE SPANISH
SETTLER AND BUILDER. THICK WALLS OF DOUBLE ADOBE THAT WERE BUILT
AS PROTECTION FROM WEATHER AND INTRUDERS ALSO OFFER A PROFOUND SENSE OF
SOLIDITY. THIS IS A HOME MADE TO LAST FOR GENERATIONS.

OPPOSITE: A broad portal, with plenty of room for sitting and watching the grass grow, is punctuated by windows and doors, multiple openings that give easy access to the outside. ABOVE: In the kitchen, as elsewhere in the home, numerous collections make a strong statement on the red shelving. A small fireplace is integrated directly into the cabinets.

BELOW: A quiet corner provides for spiritual renewal, with a collection of crosses and a beautiful folk image of the Virgin. OPPOSITE, LEFT: Old houses need big old cabinets for storage space, since closets are a relatively recent addition to home-building. Here, a big cupboard, or *trastero,* with whimsical molding and great color provides plenty of space. OPPOSITE, RIGHT: A large sculpture of the Crucifixion with a smaller *bulto,* or carved figure, of St. Anthony of Padua below, flanked by candles. Religious images were always plentiful in Hispanic homes; today, many of them are treasured antiques.

ABOVE: An area designed for dining has an overhead fan for comfort's sake. Old vines
fill the space between the supporting posts and provide more shade and a wild green screen.
OPPOSITE: Plain white linens and classic Mexican and New Mexican furniture make
a simple but bold statement in a bedroom with high ceilings and thick, tan adobe walls.

The Fine Art of Living on Canyon Road

Time was when poor artists and simple farmers lived together along a little road that headed up the canyon. Today, Canyon Road is filled with homes converted into galleries, and the rural farming life once so prevalent is gone. Few folks now can afford to live on this little road that is still so rural in feel, but Nedra and Richard Matteucci are fortunate to own a nineteenth-century dwelling known as the Prada home. Once the residence of Margretta S. Dietrich, an early founder of the preservation movement in Santa Fe, it has long been considered one of the most original houses on Canyon Road. The Matteuccis have brought their own artistic energy to the property through their beautiful landscaping and the excellent art they have acquired.

OPPOSITE: One of Santa Fe's most beloved and most photographed guest houses is cherished for its sweet proportions, its charming shutters, and the integration of its *horno*, an outdoor oven, directly into its walls.
RIGHT: The fireplace in a small formal living room has built-in *nichos* and is flanked by *bancos*. BELOW LEFT: An entry is created by the side wall of a fireplace. Around the fireplace, an exceptional collection of Native American art. BELOW RIGHT: A small group of potted flowers against the bright blue wall of the front portal.

BELOW: The dining room has deep windows
facing south, and its own corner fireplace.
RIGHT: One corner of the kitchen has not only
a fireplace—the home has many—
but also a collection of all things piggy.

ABOVE: Collections fill the home, with fine Pueblo pottery and other Native American art as well as excellent examples of Spanish colonial religious art. LEFT: A detail of Spanish colonial religious art, including carved saint figures, candlesticks, and crosses.

Collecting Native American Art

The Santa Fe home untouched by the influence of Native American art is simply unimaginable. Shelves filled with Pueblo pots, bold Navajo textiles on the floor, Indian designs on everything from furniture to walls—these elements have been directly incorporated into the Santa Fe home for hundreds of years by all segments of the population. Pueblo pottery, in particular, with its ancient traditions and ongoing development has offered an enormous repository of design motifs. Navajo blankets, America's premier contribution to textile design, are perhaps of equal influence, their colors and patterns setting a standard of bold elegance that adds beauty to any setting, and again find echoes in countless designs.

ABOVE LEFT: A series of simple contemporary headdresses, used in ceremonial dances, fills a staircase wall. ABOVE RIGHT: Hopi kachinas, or ceremonial figures, and a pair of Pueblo moccasins sit upon an elegant old grain chest. RIGHT: Collections of Southwestern Navajo jewelry of turquoise, shell, and silver not only serve as personal adornment but are also hung as works of art. OPPOSITE, TOP LEFT: A grouping of witty turkeys and other fowl—all Pueblo figurative pottery— keep company with a lamp. OPPOSITE, TOP RIGHT: Fine examples of Pueblo pottery upon a fireplace mantel. OPPOSITE, BOTTOM: One corner of this home shows an amazing assortment of Native American art, some fine, some fun.

Skulls

With their empty sockets and gleaming white surfaces, steer skulls have long been emblematic of the old West. They evoke images of dry and empty spaces, of the sudden cruelty of nature, the loneliness of the ranching experience, and much more, but it took an artist to focus our vision upon their beauty. Georgia O'Keeffe's skulls floating in the blue New Mexican sky or beribboned with morning glories captured the stark contrasts found in these most organic objects. She collected the rocks and bones and weird desiccated woods that she found around her Abiquiu home. Some she saved throughout her life, integrating them into her home and her art. Despite the importance she placed upon maintaining her privacy, the images O'Keeffe created of New Mexico's beauty permeate regional design, influencing forever our experience of the land. To some degree, the skulls we place on our walls and above our fireplaces to guard our homes transcend their original links to the ranching West, and serve as an homage to an artist whose influence is so strongly felt.

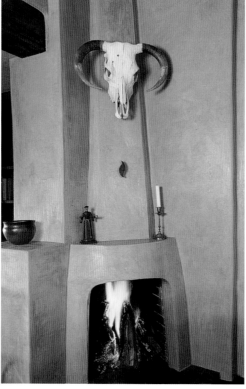

ABOVE: A gallery of deer, steer, and other skulls on a garage door in Taos. OPPOSITE, TOP: A stark white skull against an adobe fireplace wall is being gradually covered with morning glories. OPPOSITE, BOTTOM LEFT: Above a table on a porch, this found skull makes its resting place. OPPOSITE, BOTTOM RIGHT: As a small corner fireplace blazes below, the skull of a steer keeps its silent vigil. It is not unusual to find skulls in almost any room in Santa Fe, including the bedroom.

FIRE

The fiery colors of red, yellow, and orange light up the fall.
Santa Feans head for the hills to gather in the brilliance of the season and live
in their kitchens, enjoying the bounty of the harvest.

Santa Fe is located in the foothills of the Rockies as they tumble down to their dramatic finale, the Sangre de Cristo Mountains. Besides suggesting the deep religious faith of the Spanish settlers, the name of these mountains—"Blood of Christ"—also evokes the bloodred sunsets that reflect off the snow-covered mountains from fall into spring. We are of fire here, with our red chiles, our blazing state flag of red on yellow, glowing red-rock mesas, and our fires literally in every corner of the house. Our shelters are hearth-centered, each room focusing on the creation and preservation of heat. Low ceilings, corner fireplaces, thick adobe walls, small windows, modest doorways, and piles and piles of piñon pine stacked beneath protecting porches—all reflect life in the high desert. With our own distinct cuisine—defined by our state's perennial question, Red or green chile?—we live in our kitchens. Like everything else in Santa Fe culture, we are drawn to the basics, characterized by the simple and direct. The chile is hot, the fire pungent, the air crisp and defined, the walls thick and sheltering. Santa Fe was born not of subtlety but of bravura.

A contemporary *santo* by a local Hispanic artist represents the Holy Child. The figure sits in a *nicho* painted brilliant red.

ABOVE: An altar prepared for the Mexican celebration of the Days of the Dead—All Saints' and All Souls' Days— features traditional marigolds and coxcomb. LEFT: A detail of harvest foods placed upon the altar. FAR LEFT: Fields of yellow wildflowers appear in the fall. OPPOSITE, TOP LEFT: A harvest of marigolds ready to decorate the altar. OPPOSITE, TOP RIGHT: A bright red sunset highlights each spine of the cholla cactus. RIGHT: A dramatic example of how the Sangre de Cristo Mountains got their name.

FALL

The time of year most cherished and celebrated, fall is Santa Fe's best season. Almost every day brings bright blue skies and deep yellow leaves to contrast with drying strings of chiles. The beauty of the season is heightened by its transience—life at seven thousand feet defies predictability. This gives autumn a somewhat frantic feeling. Farmers and gardeners must rush to gather in the harvest, yet also give their crops a chance for full maturity. And, we rush to embrace the incredible mutable beauty so dramatically laid out before us. Each cottonwood tree calls for our attention, while wild asters from the roadsides and flaming red leaves here and there demand their due. We try to gather it all in before it passes.

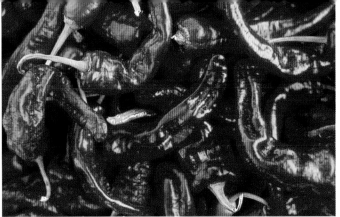

OPPOSITE: Some reds provided by the bold graphics of a railroad car and a pickup truck. The brilliant colors of the harvest are used to adorn home and vehicle alike.

Fireplaces

The humble little fireplaces of Santa Fe are so ubiquitous as to become almost invisible to residents, yet they hardly occur any other place in the country. It is their structure and placement that distinguishes them. Found most frequently in room corners, their soft funnel-like shape and gently curved openings have no equivalent in the squared-off structures found elsewhere. There were, and are, endless variations on the basic structure of the corner fireplace, since each is a handmade part of the home—a building task that traditionally fell to the women. The contemporary jargon of the region labels them "kiva fireplaces," as if their origin was somehow tied to the ceremonial structures of Native Americans. But their true origin is Spanish, and most likely Arabic, since they share much of their style, structure, and function with our outdoor ovens, the *horno,* also derived from North Africa. Once used for cooking in addition to heating, their modest appearance belies their wonderful efficiency. Like so much else in the Santa Fe home, they are models of hard work and simplicity. On their triangulated hearths, the cook can rest a small trivet upon which a pot or a round griddle, known as a *comal,* could be placed.

Like the fireplace itself, even our fires have a style of their own (Is there no element of life untouched by Santa Fe's idiosyncrasy?). Forget the andirons; fires here are built vertically, not horizontally, using fast-burning woods to heat the back wall. Slower-burning, harder-to-ignite woods, and such "cracklers" as juniper are then added. Once well lit, these little corner fireplaces can nicely heat up thick adobe walls and keep small rooms warm. Small windows and low ceilings and doorways work together to retain heat. More formal spaces, such as living rooms, often feature

The large central fireplace in this living room matches the scale of the space. Above the fireplace an impressive crucifix done in the nineteenth century by a New Mexican *santero,* or saint maker. The fireplace is flanked by a collection of paintings of New Mexican subjects from the first half of the twentieth century.

central fireplaces. Though more conventional compared to the corner fireplaces, they, too, display regional tastes. Framed with wooden surrounds in styles first introduced during New Mexico's Territorial Period or built out of locally available stone or plaster, these large fireplaces still reflect the area because they are made with indigenous materials, using traditional styles.

RIGHT: A style of fireplace rarely found, but much beloved, is the shepherd's fireplace. The hearth extends to one side so that cooking equipment, such as trivets and pots, can be accommodated. A plastered shelf lies over the extended hearth, while the hood sits only above the firebox. It is the shelf that gives the fireplace its name, since it was used by shepherds for sleeping. The shelf also held food, especially for drying. OPPOSITE, TOP LEFT: The sculptural lines of this fireplace add beauty to the room even in the summer months. OPPOSITE, TOP RIGHT: An elaborate contemporary dance *tablita* above a fireplace, with examples of Mexican folk art below. OPPOSITE, BOTTOM RIGHT: A fireplace in a quiet setting. OPPOSITE, BOTTOM LEFT: This little fireplace sits not three feet away as I write. It is located in the former grist room of El Molinito, the Little Mill, which is on Acequia Madre and is the oldest mill in town. The fireplace here was built in the mid-twentieth century by an unknown Native American artisan. The little angels and the saint figures below were carved by the late Alex Sandoval, a regional folk artist. To the right of the fireplace, a little Pueblo pot has been plastered into the wall to hold matches.

LEFT: A trim and chaste fireplace, designed by architect John Gaw Meem in the 1950s, is located in a front entryway. Note the fire screen with the figures of the firewood seller and his burros. BELOW: One corner of a kitchen has a fireplace with a hood, incorporating heavy cedar branches. This fireplace was designed by Carlos Vierra, Santa Fe's first resident artist at the turn of the twentieth century. OPPOSITE, TOP LEFT: A Native American artist has painted a fireplace surround in the same style as the Pueblo pottery of the region. OPPOSITE, TOP RIGHT: A bright white plaster surround contrasts with the adobe-colored walls to make an elegant statement. OPPOSITE, BOTTOM RIGHT: A plain plastered fireplace in the living room of a Meem-designed home has a wooden mantel that serves to display a collection of Pueblo pottery.

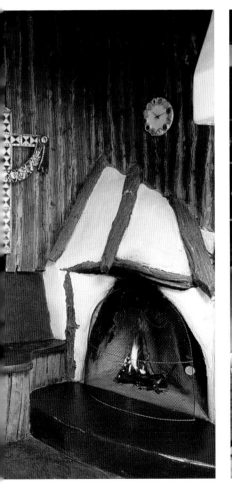

Firewood

Santa Fe once boasted an alley entirely given over to the sale of firewood and to the little burros that brought the wood to town—Burro Alley. Today, the burros are absent from our streets but we still love a wood fire, especially one burning our sweet-smelling piñon wood.

An evening walk can be filled with the distinct piñon fragrance that is Santa Fe's signature perfume. But now we pick up a cord from vendors along the Old Las Vegas Highway or head over to Mr. Rios's yard on Camino del Monte Sol, where the stacks of split wood could make a fire marshal's heart stop.

ABOVE: By summer, the stack of firewood by the front door has been almost used up. Soon, it will be time to lay in the wood for another winter. OPPOSITE: An ingenious little fireplace has a flagstone hearth and a well-designed space below for firewood and kindling.

Kitchens

Early kitchens had few utensils and only the simplest of ingredients; their owners relied upon the open hearth for warmth and cooking. These little kitchens of the past still set the standard for those of Santa Fe, where the focus is upon the fireplace and stove and the emphasis is upon simple preparations and the use of the kitchen as a family gathering place. Many of these kitchens contain collections of earthenware pottery, sturdy wooden tools, solid stoves, and personal whimsies—some stored in great old cupboards, or *trasteros*. First among regional cuisine, Santa Fe cooking relies upon New World plants—corn, chile, beans, and squash—combined with Old World foods and preparations. Strong, and sometimes fiery, foods form not just the basis of our daily meals, but also seem to define the look of our kitchens. There is a sense of the farmhouse here. It's a place where large pots can simmer for long periods of time. There is a constant shortage of space, with full larders and eclectic kitchen collections vying for room and both spilling out onto the counters. It is here that the personality of the cook is often most evident. Our kitchens have color, whimsy, and humor, as the irrepressible spirit of our town cozies into the wood, adobe, and warmth.

LEFT: A pitched roof, beams, and a big table for both eating and working makes this room the center of activity.
ABOVE: A mustard-yellow stove brings great cheer to this corner of my kitchen. In front, one of the many chickens made by the Navajo artists of the Yazzie-Herbert family that have invaded the Mather home. The framed tiles are vintage examples purchased in Puebla, Mexico. Behind the stove are plain, small Saltillo tiles.

ABOVE: This bricked-in alcove for the stove serves not only to frame the stove, but also to vent it. In addition, its shape mimics old country kitchens with their broad and deep hearths. RIGHT: Patterned tile from Italy and open glass fronts on the cabinets brighten this corner of the kitchen. OPPOSITE, TOP: A plastered and hand-painted range hood extends across the grill and stove, and in the center sits a rooster by folk artist David Alvarez. OPPOSITE, BOTTOM: White walls and cabinets, dark floors, and lots of green set this kitchen apart. The ceramics hanging on the range hood and above the counter are part of a much larger collection of vintage Oaxacan pieces, all in green and white.

OPPOSITE, TOP LEFT: Divided by ceiling beams, a big open kitchen with room for everyone to gather. OPPOSITE, TOP RIGHT: A detail of the kitchen shows that chickens rule the roost. OPPOSITE, BELOW: This kitchen offers great space for sitting and working. The plastered walls with their high polished finish bring reflected light into the rooms, as does a skylight set between the *vigas*. BELOW: Blue cabinets have inset panels of punched tin done by a local Hispanic artisan. Above the cabinets is a collection of Hopi kachinas.

Chickens are here, they're there, they're everywhere! They seem to be a design favorite here and have insinuated themselves into many a Santa Fe home. OPPOSITE: Navajo chickens by the Yazzie-Herbert family strut their stuff out in front of their Four Corners home on the Navajo reservation. ABOVE: A mad-looking blue chicken on a post in the garden. RIGHT: A wall of shelves filled with chicken pots from Mexico. These vintage pieces were originally designed for cooking but rapidly became more decorative than utilitarian. BELOW: Chickens in my kitchen. LEFT: A blessedly silent chicken from Mexico, made by the Medrano family, near Guadalajara.

Painted Walls

Wall painting in New Mexico is a tradition that spans many hundreds of years, from prehistoric structures to contemporary homes. There are walls that tell a story; there are walls that are flights of fancy; there are walls that appear to be things they are not; there are bright, zingy walls and soft, earthy walls; and each adds to Santa Fe's reputation for individualism. That a person might make of his dwelling not a castle but a canvas is so widely accepted as to appear to be the norm. Santa Feans are not shy about trying new colors, adding decoration to the fireplace, window, or doorway, or bringing a touch of frivolity to a mailbox or windowpane.

Native American ceremonial buildings had painted walls that told stories that were passed down over the centuries. Churches from New Mexico's early colonial era frequently had wall paintings as well, sometimes to mimic elaborate finishes or else to convey the symbols and stories of Christianity to the newly converted. Interiors of adobe homes were often whitewashed to add reflected light with decorative dados of paint or even patterned fabrics to make the rooms more livable and beautiful. Anglo-American artists enthusiastically tried their hands at adding decorative elements to their homes, and some went on to create the public murals that remain an important part of New Mexico's artistic legacy. Simple stenciled decorations can be found around windows and doors in many Santa Fe homes, frequently using decorative elements of Native American pottery or early colonial art.

OPPOSITE: An artist's home has bright banners of color throughout, as in this dining room. The colors are offset by white walls elsewhere. BELOW: In the bedroom, folk colors of violet and red make the art on the walls sing.

ABOVE AND RIGHT: Specially commissioned decorative wall paintings above a doorway and in an alcove room just off the kitchen focus upon the bounties of food. The saint figure is of San Pascual, the one who guards and blesses the kitchen. OPPOSITE, TOP RIGHT: A red mottled wall and a handcrafted chair with designs painted to match. OPPOSITE, BOTTOM RIGHT: Morning glories wind their way up from the windowsill. OPPOSITE, LEFT: A *nicho* in a dining room has many uses; it provides storage, can be used as a serving area, and is a shrine. The red wall behind the central image of the Virgin, from Mexico, highlights the painting with its painted glass and tin frame.

SAN PASCUAL BAILÓN

ABOVE: Coral-colored walls behind the shelves serve to emphasize the wonderful folk quality of this room with its many collections. FAR LEFT: Not all painting is on the walls, as demonstrated in this white floor with red-and-blue stenciled design. LEFT: Around a door, lots of design and bright color. OPPOSITE: Paint and paper make this bathroom wall a shiny backdrop to a collection of Japanese folk art. The wall is covered with squares of gold paper.

Dining Rooms

Dining rooms in Santa Fe homes tend to be among the more formal areas of the house, though meals are also taken home-style in the kitchen, with elbows upon the table. This duality of elegant and formal versus simple and loose can be found in home after home, suggesting that we like dining both ways. Of course, formality in Santa Fe is a relative thing. Long wooden tables from colonial Mexico are highly prized additions to dining rooms. With their uneven surfaces and look of enormous usage, they fit right into our homes. The proportions—long and narrow—are made for big groups of people who like sitting face to face, and make for long nights of conversation and food. Family heirlooms tend to drift toward the dining room, meaning that great old English and American tables and chairs can be found in the long and high rooms of adobe and beams. Upon the table is inevitably an eclectic mix of local crafts, fine antiques, flowers, textiles from all over, and Grandma's silver—anything goes. But when not planning for a big sit-down, we take our meals in the kitchen. Here a well-defined space with a mix of chairs or a *banco* and a view to the garden or the mountains makes simple meals a pleasure. And regardless of where in the home we choose to eat, there is sure to be a fireplace— big, square, and formal or small and tucked into the corner.

A classic dining room open to a living room features a big Mexican bench, with a scalloped profile, on one side as seating.

TOP LEFT AND TOP CENTER: Two different examples of how well American and European antiques fit into old adobe homes. This is perhaps because Santa Fe homes, with their beamed ceilings, are reminiscent of those found in rural areas throughout Europe. The proportions are classic, the walls thick and substantial, and the emphasis is upon utility and simplicity. TOP RIGHT: An unusual door frame and corner fireplace provide all of the decoration needed in this lovely little room. FAR RIGHT, MIDDLE: Within a big country kitchen a *banco* and corner fireplace add immeasurably to the beauty and comfort of the small dining area. FAR RIGHT, BOTTOM: A generous *banco* provides most of the seating in this room off the kitchen, designed for casual dining. BOTTOM CENTER: One corner of a substantial dining room reveals a modest plastered fireplace with a portrait painting above. BOTTOM LEFT: An extraordinary Spanish colonial painting of Our Lady the Divine Shepherdess dominates the dining room of a collector of colonial Latin American art. Some of the ceramics on the shelves are from the same period in colonial history.

At Home in Santa Fe

ONCE ONE HOME, THEN TWO HOMES, AND FINALLY BROUGHT BACK TOGETHER AGAIN BY THE CURRENT
OWNERS, THIS ADOBE RAMBLES IN A MOST DELIGHTFUL WAY. THE FORMER RESIDENCE OF THE LATE
LAURA GILPIN, FAMED SOUTHWESTERN PHOTOGRAPHER, IT HAS BEEN GIVEN AN ADVENTUROUS NEW
LIFE BY THE INCLUSION OF PAINTED WALLS AND AN OUTSTANDING MIX OF FINE AND FOLK ART.

ABOVE: A dining area contains a *nicho* with a folk image of a seated Mexican man and a group of painted chests from the Michoacán and Uruapan areas of Mexico. The glass-and-tin cross would have been used in a Mexican church and carried in procession. The painting, probably Mexican, is a *bodegón,* a type of still life where objects carry great symbolic significance. LEFT: A door-framing device designed by Deena Perry. OPPOSITE: A *sala*-style living room with a central fireplace. The room also serves as a hallway to the rooms beyond.

ABOVE: A fiery red room has a corner fireplace to add even more warmth, and white woodwork for contrast. OPPOSITE, RIGHT: A carved figure of St. Anthony and the Christ Child rests upon an old Mexican table; the *nicho* shows St. Francis, the patron saint of Santa Fe, in his study. OPPOSITE, TOP LEFT: A dining area decorated completely with Mexican folk art, including a set of paintings that are still lifes of kitchen cupboards. OPPOSITE, BOTTOM LEFT: A detail of the corner fireplace, with three Mexican ladies'-face pitchers from the turn of the twentieth century.

Angels of Clay Within

THE CLAY ANGEL IS A MECCA FOR THOSE WHO LOVE CERAMICS. THE OWNERS HAVE BROUGHT THE VIVID COLORS OF MEDITERRANEAN AND LATIN CERAMICS TO THE WALLS AND SHELVES OF THEIR HOME. THE DILLENBERGS' OLD ADOBE, ORIGINALLY PURCHASED AND RENOVATED BY ARTIST GERALD CASSIDY AND HIS WIFE, INA SIZER CASSIDY— AMONG THE FIRST ARTISTS IN SANTA FE—WAS ALSO THE FIRST ARTIST RESIDENCE ON CANYON ROAD. THE DILLENBERGS HONOR THEIR LEGACY BY WELCOMING THE ARTISTIC COMMUNITY TO THE HOUSE, ESPECIALLY THOSE WHO SHARE THEIR PASSION FOR CERAMICS.

RIGHT: A large formal entryway. BELOW: A face pot by a door that leads to the entryway.

ABOVE: Green walls serve as a bright backdrop for saint figures, many by the regional artist Anita Romero Jones. The table holds a small part of the collection brought together by the owners of the Clay Angel, as they track down sources throughout Europe and beyond. OPPOSITE: In the front hallway, beams and an old door, which are integrated into the wall, frame a group of *retablos*, or paintings of saint figures, from the Spanish colonial period, painted on both wood and tin.

ABOVE: Viewed from the living room to the front hallway, the beams and corbels, originally taken from a destroyed church at Nambe, New Mexico, act as frames. The corner fireplace displays a collection of Spanish colonial religious art. OPPOSITE, TOP LEFT: A small carved door with a built-in cupboard and a *nicho* above. OPPOSITE, TOP RIGHT: Like many small corner fireplaces, this one functions as a display area, as a source of heat, and as a transition point between two rooms. OPPOSITE, BOTTOM: A carved and painted figure of St. John the Baptist is from the colonial Spanish era, as are the two candle sconces.

Ceramics

Inside and out, painted and plain, utilitarian and decorative, delicate and massive, Native American, Mexican, Spanish, Italian, Portuguese, Arabic, and more, in pieces or whole, potter's wares can be found in almost every Santa Fe home. This is a town filled with potters and it has a long history of importing pottery. We eat out of pots, stick our plants in them, and carefully collect them. Often it is in pottery that we find our greatest artistic solace and inspiration. Mexican pottery is almost as important as our New Mexican ceramics. Imported to our region hundreds of years ago along the Camino Real, it continues to influence our taste in colors and patterns. The ceramic products of other parts of Latin America, as well as Old World ceramics, also make their way into our homes. Craft work, after all, is a significant element in the design repertoire of the community, and potters continue to be among our most widely respected artists, adding to and borrowing from our long artisanal history.

TOP: Small plates, largely from the Oaxaca area of Mexico, are part of a collection of vintage Mexican pottery. ABOVE: A rare example of colonial Mexican pottery made prior to the 1820s, this type of tableware was preferred by Spanish colonists over indigenous pottery. LEFT: A brilliant red, white, and blue motif on a Mexican colonial plate. OPPOSITE: A ceramic shrine from Europe with the figure of the Virgin; in front, a small figure of the Christ Child in wood.

Creating Anew to Follow the Old

WHAT APPEARS TO BE A GRAND OLD ADOBE, WITH THICK WALLS AND CURVING SPACES, IS ACTUALLY
MADE OF STRAW BALES. STANDARD BALES OF STRAW ARE INCREASINGLY BEING USED TO CREATE
HOMES THAT HAVE THE SAME FEEL AND PROPORTIONS OF THE EARTHEN STRUCTURES. THIS TECHNOLOGY
ALLOWS NEW HOME BUILDERS TO CAPTURE THE ORGANIC SPIRIT OF THE BIG OLD ADOBES.

ABOVE: Shutters, old farm implements, and painted furniture give the front portal a rustic look. This home is located just southeast of the city in Arroyo Hondo, a rural area with wide vistas to the south. OPPOSITE: Walls give protection to the front portal. Their thick proportions are highlighted by the buttresses beside the gate that was salvaged from Mexico.

ABOVE: A series of photographic prints by Edward Curtis lines the stairway as it gently curves upward to a bedroom above. OPPOSITE, TOP: The dining area with its graceful coved ceiling and thick walls is both welcoming and grand. OPPOSITE, BOTTOM RIGHT: A *nicho* with a plaster-framing device goes through the wall to the hallway beyond. OPPOSITE, BOTTOM CENTER: The coved ceiling is emphasized by the contrast between wall and ceiling colors. RIGHT: A detail of the dining room with mottled and painted wall surface accented by the long, old Mexican table.

TOP LEFT: A skylight in the front hall illuminates a simple chair. TOP CENTER: A detail of the *nicho* in the dining room. ABOVE RIGHT: An elevated and very sensuous corner fireplace in the bedroom has a flagstone hearth and room below for a small stack of firewood. ABOVE LEFT: In a child's room, simple blue shutters and blue quilts impart a Shaker-like purity. OPPOSITE: Above the bench in the front entryway, a trompe l'oeil painting with shutters opening to an imaginary view beyond. Curved arches reaching into the hall emphasize the wall's depth.

Dearly Beloved

A HOME BUILT BY COAUTHOR SHARON WOODS FOR SANDY AND
RUSSELL OSTERMAN IS DEAR TO BOTH THE OWNERS AND THE
BUILDER, SINCE IT SO CLEARLY DEMONSTRATES A MEETING OF THE
MINDS. THE HOME, WHILE CLEARLY NEW, SPEAKS OF DEVOTION TO
THE PAST AND TO THE CLASSIC ELEMENTS OF OUR REGIONAL STYLE.
ONE LARGE ROOM DOMINATES THE CENTER OF THE HOUSE. ALL
THE ROOMS HAVE THE ADVANTAGE OF THE STUNNING VIEWS
THAT SURROUND THE HOME.

ABOVE: The living room with its large arched windows and thick adobe
walls is a warm, inviting space even though it is somewhat formal.
Smaller areas within the space encourage conversation; the room also
benefits from wonderful proportions. OPPOSITE, LEFT: Above a Mexican
vestry table, the remains of a carved and painted altar are used
as a backdrop for a group of *santos*, from Mexico and New Mexico.
OPPOSITE, TOP RIGHT: A large *trastero* in the living room has Mexican
religious paintings inset within the front panels. OPPOSITE, BOTTOM
RIGHT: A detail of the carved stone mantel with a saint figure above.

OPPOSITE: The master bedroom looks to the Sangre de Cristo Mountains. Simple surfaces and furnishings throughout the house allow the proportions of the rooms to dominate. ABOVE: Texture and color from an old table and a few faux flowers located in the living room are details that bring calm to the space. ABOVE RIGHT: Filigree ironwork set in a shuttered frame offers a view from the dining area to the living room below. RIGHT: The Virgin and Child are the main focus in an altarlike setting in the living room.

OPPOSITE, TOP LEFT: The blue guest bathroom continues the mood of calm and devotion. OPPOSITE, TOP CENTER: In the dining room, a large *nicho* holds Latin American religious art. OPPOSITE, TOP RIGHT: An old wash table contains a sink. OPPOSITE, BOTTOM: The front portal of the guest house has been arranged with a table and chairs and plenty of firewood so that the outside corner fireplace can be enjoyed. LEFT: A small arched stairway leads to a study, giving the space a monastic look. BELOW: In the sitting room, a corner fireplace is given a tall wooden surround.

Bancos

Bancos are simply benches, but our benches are more than places to sit. They hold a special place in the hearts of Santa Feans. They have often traveled long distances, been painted numerous times, weathered abuse, neglect, and bird droppings, yet maintain their craggy dignity as survivors. Along with old crusty six-board chests and elegant tall cupboards, our benches are dear to us. Migrating from porches to hallways, living rooms to kitchens, they add solidity and beauty to each location. Some are old Mexican in origin, some Spanish; a few are colonial New Mexican; others are flea-market finds of unknown lineage. Many have remarkable patinas that create gorgeous backdrops for regional textiles. Besides benches of solid pine and fading paint, Santa Feans can also create furniture from the very mud of their walls—one or more layers of adobe bricks covered in plaster can make a *banco*. Walls that morph into furniture, including cupboards, *nichos*, and benches, demonstrate the tremendous creativity and practicality emanating from the humble adobe home.

OPPOSITE: A fine colonial Mexican bench with an iron cross and symbols of the Passion. Pillows and a cushion provide comfort. TOP LEFT: With wreaths of small red chiles, a well-used and frequently painted bench on a front porch is ready for Christmas. TOP RIGHT: An adobe *banco* in a kitchen has enough cushions so that the cook will always have plenty of company. RIGHT: A built-in *banco* with a shelf above. ABOVE: Above the scalloped backrest of this Mexican bench is a grouping of folk figures from Mexico, representing the Seven Deadly Sins.

Hardware and Metalwork

The decorative ironwork of Santa Fe homes has a simple honest appeal, adding visual strength and practical beauty to homes and furniture. Doors especially are vehicles for the special decorative touches of the ironworker. Iron was among the most highly valued materials of the colonial home in New Mexico, in part because of its extreme rarity, but primarily because of its tenacious practicality. Ironworkers accompanied all early expeditions, for without their fix-it talents, plans would quickly evaporate. Without iron tools and weapons, the colonial enterprise would have been impossible.

As a decorative element in New Mexico, iron and other metalwork retains its prestige. Wonderful decorative grills adorn interior windows, showing off the ironworker's skills. With their taste for the bold, Santa Feans favor hinges and lock plates that dominate the plain surfaces of much furniture. Ironwork captures the combination of great practicality, hard physical labor, and striking decorative elements that typifies so many homes in Santa Fe.

TOP LEFT: A home dedicated to the popular saint San Isidro Labrador has specially carved lock plates on the doors. TOP RIGHT: A very well-weathered lock plate and handle on an equally well-weathered gate. LEFT: A detail of the filigreed ironwork on a grill panel shows the intricate patterns created. OPPOSITE, LEFT: Seen from the other side, this same grill panel of filigreed ironwork shows the skills of a master craftsman. OPPOSITE, TOP RIGHT: A small knob to open and close the damper on a corner fireplace casts beautiful curling shadows upon a white plaster surface. OPPOSITE, BOTTOM RIGHT: The rusting remains of an ornamental cross.

ABOVE: An electrified chandelier is based directly on early fixtures that held candles. The simple stamped and punched decoration on the dull tin surface makes for an attractive traditional statement.

Lighting in Tin

Even though modernization came to New Mexico by the twentieth century, there was a continued reliance on local traditional styles so that new technologies were often given the look of the old. An interest in maintaining or reviving traditional crafts animated the newly arrived arts community. Besides creating an early historic preservation movement to save adobe monuments, artists also encouraged craftsmen to update traditional crafts for so-called modern homes. With the advent of the WPA in New Mexico, traditional crafts for making furniture, textiles, religious art, and tinwork were all revived, and outlets were created so that homeowners would have access to these decorative arts. Lighting especially benefited from this revival period, with traditional forms like punched-tin fixtures getting electrified. Workshops produced fixtures for hotels, businesses, and homes, giving each a distinct regional look based on old craft styles. Tin craftsmen continue to provide special fixtures for our homes, adding to the repertoire of styles in this humble but highly effective art.

OPPOSITE, BOTTOM: This large tin-and-painted-glass revival fixture was probably made for a hotel lobby or hallway, given its proportions. The form is based upon the tin-and-glass *nichos* made to hold saint figures, which were popular with the Hispanic population in the last half of the nineteenth century. LEFT: Besides providing soft illumination, the reflected light from this tin-and-glass Mexican sconce throws decorative patterns upon the walls. BELOW: A new chandelier continues to use traditional designs in such decorative elements as the rosette.

The Artists Within

A VERY OLD ADOBE BECOMES A LARGE THREE-DIMENSIONAL WORK OF ART FOR SCULPTOR LUIS TAPIA AND WRITER CARMELLA PADILLA. THIS HUSBAND-AND-WIFE TEAM IS DEEPLY INVOLVED IN THE TRADITIONAL REPRESENTATIONS OF NORTHERN NEW MEXICAN CULTURE AS WELL AS BEING PEOPLE OF CONTEMPORARY ARTISTIC SENSIBILITIES. CAREFULLY NURTURING A GRADUAL COLLECTION OF BOTH TRADITIONAL WORKS AND CONTEMPORARY PIECES BY FELLOW ARTISTS, THEY HAVE CREATED A HOME FILLED WITH THE SPIRIT OF NEW MEXICO.

OPPOSITE, TOP LEFT: A door, a floor, and a fireplace, with signature New Mexican blues. OPPOSITE, BOTTOM LEFT: Another view of the bedroom reveals a large contemporary crucifixion and simple furnishings. LEFT: The deep doorways and uneven floors of this old home lead to a room beyond with a large cupboard. On the wall in the foreground is the scalloped edging of a traditional *repisa*, or shelf.

ABOVE: An old wood-burning stove is the primary work of art in the kitchen. A deep window is framed with plain molding painted black. OPPOSITE, TOP LEFT: The blue corner fireplace, with some examples of Luis Tapia's work. OPPOSITE, BOTTOM LEFT: A vintage cut-and-painted tin rack holds a group of vintage Mexican pottery cups. OPPOSITE, RIGHT: A broad hallway divides the house; against the back wall hangs a collection of Mexican masks.

ABOVE LEFT: A large *nicho* with lighting from above was created especially for this large religious sculpture of Our Lady of Sorrows, carved and painted by Felix Lopez. ABOVE RIGHT: An entire door becomes a type of *retablo,* with its religious folk images painted in the style of the old New Mexican works on wood. OPPOSITE, LEFT: Below the kitchen counter in the Mahaffey home, a painting by Sergio Tapia combines an old subject—the churches of New Mexico—with other locally sacred images—low-rider vehicles. OPPOSITE, RIGHT: Illuminated from behind, this outdoor shrine to the Virgin of Guadalupe is painted on glass by artist Luis Tapia.

Collecting Devotional Art

Traditional Hispanic crafts and religious art were in sharp decline by the late nineteenth century with the importation of manufactured goods into the region. An active revival of craft in the 1930s gave the work new impetus, although by the 1960s much of this energy had faded. During the 1970s, another, less traditional group of artists began to revive the old techniques, while integrating new social currents into their art. The annual Spanish Market, held on Santa Fe's Plaza in July, grew both in size and in spirit during this period, making Hispanic art an important avenue of expression for the community.

Devotion—whether to higher powers, ancestors, or holy experiences—is an aspect of Santa Fe life that finds visual expression in almost every home. Religious expression can be found in the ubiquitous collections of reliquaries, saint figures, crosses, candles, and

ABOVE: A small bedroom with a door painted with various figures of archangels and a small *nicho* with a figure of St. Francis by the late, beloved folk carver Benjamin Ortega. RIGHT: A *nicho* painted with a celestial motif includes an image of the Holy Spirit, and contains a few colonial New Mexican religious figures. OPPOSITE, TOP: A large painting of the Virgin from the elegant Cuzco school of painting from colonial Peru. OPPOSITE, BOTTOM LEFT: A painting of the young Virgin dominates a living room.

votive offerings. Rooms for devotional purposes and even private chapels are traditional to New Mexican homes, as are small spaces set aside for moments of worship. Among the Spanish, all art tended to be religious in nature and the legacy of this pervades contemporary life in New Mexico. Collectors can find a wealth of items dedicated to particular saints and holy figures, and collections of saint figures from throughout the Latin American world are found in many homes.

BELOW: A remarkably intact cross with the symbols of the Passion is an outstanding folk piece from late-nineteenth- or early-twentieth-century Peru. Tiny mirrors along the vertical connecting elements would have provided sparkling beams of light in a dark church or home shrine.

Dedicated to Devotion

THE HOME OF ASHLEY AND PAUL MARGETSON REVEALS THEIR EVER-EXPANDING INTEREST IN
RELIGIOUS FOLK ART. RATHER THAN CONVEYING A PIOUS SENSIBILITY, THIS IS AN ECLECTIC HOME
FILLED WITH WHIMSICAL JUXTAPOSITIONS AND PLAYFUL ALLIANCES.

OPPOSITE: The front entryway opens up to a dining area—bathed in light from above and filled with hanging paper banners from Mexico. ABOVE LEFT: The large entry door is colonial Mexican and includes a smaller door within for easier access. ABOVE RIGHT: An arched doorway with a plaster surround leads to a library below. LEFT: The tub area has a wall that might be described as an altar for ancestor worship, since it is filled with hundreds of little framed photos of family.

ABOVE: The large bedstead is covered with *milagros*, or metallic devotional pieces. RIGHT: No space is without its religious figures; here a range hood serves double duty as shrine and cover. OPPOSITE, TOP: A detail shows a fraction of the religious art in this collection. OPPOSITE, BOTTOM RIGHT: An alcove in the dining room is devoted to the Margetsons' collection. Lighting from above, carved corbels and posts, and a painted wall create a striking setting. OPPOSITE, BOTTOM LEFT: A carved stone *nicho* from Mexico holds a figure of St. Anthony.

WATER

Spring in Santa Fe brings blue skies, melting snows, and quick rainstorms.
Water falls upon us, flows by us, and offers new life to our desert landscape.
We welcome it into our homes, and with it, the color blue.

The high desert seems to be lusher than it actually is, since the mountain evergreens offer visual relief from the dryness that pervades the landscape. In a desert clime nothing is more important than water. Because the melting snowfalls of the high mountains give us our water in the spring and summer months, we gauge our snows as carefully as our rains. Along the Rio Grande and its tributaries, stands of twisting cottonwoods signal the life of the river as it flows from Colorado to the Gulf of Mexico. Deep gorges and small valleys funnel the narrow ribbon of water along its course. Little towns, cities, Indian Pueblos, and farmhouses share the water in uneasy alliances, each carefully guarding its rights.

In Santa Fe, an ancient series of acequias, or irrigation ditches, long supported farms and mills. Usage rights to water from the acequias were carefully specified; woe to the users who exceeded their allotments. It is from this scarcity that the town grew first along the river and then spread outward to snake along the irrigation ditches. No house or farm was possible that did not have direct access to water, so there were water wars and water laws and bitter squabbles down through the centuries. The modest Santa Fe River is still a primary water source, along with deep wells that tap into the aquifer. In gardens, small fountains and ponds proclaim the wealth of water. Of all the elements of our lives, water has the most sensuous beauty, the most soothing and healing effects. It falls upon us, flows by us, fills and becomes us, offers us life.

Because Santa Fe is so high and dry, pools such as this one are especially inviting. With a view to the mountains beyond, this pool has a diving platform made of the local flagstone.

A variety of spring blossoms, including fruit trees and Santa Fe's famous profusion of lilacs. We may have masses of violet and reddish-blue lilacs, the sweetest fruit flowers of the apricot, apple, cherry, and crab trees, and the youngest, purest leaves of green, all against a deep blue sky.

SPRING

Spring in Santa Fe is a series of starts and stops, deep disappointments, and such piercing beauty that we forgive it the cruel taunting. In high-altitude areas, spring comes and goes—lambs and lions contest the terrain on what seems, at times, to be an hourly basis. It is a season of winds, blowing the petals off the trees, marring what might otherwise be a perfectly fine day. With the first breaths of warmth and growth, we prepare to break ground on all the projects that have been slowed by freezing temperatures. But few cities have the many dirt roads that Santa Fe has (and that Santa Feans defend and favor), so when the thaw comes, so too comes the mud; suddenly the frozen ground seems appealing. Finally the winds wick away the moisture; the trees are granted time to blossom; and the warmth from the intense spring sun seeps into the earth so that the season can unfold—at least until the next storm.

Blue

We like our blues, be they turquoise or cobalt, faded-robin's-egg or deep navy. There is talk that Santa Fe's blue doorways and window sashes are historically related to the blue garments of the Franciscan friars who once offered security and solace to many. No matter where the roots of this attachment lie, one cannot quite imagine a street side in Santa Fe without a bit of blue showing around the edges of windows and doors.

ABOVE RIGHT: A highly prized vehicle in the quintessential color. RIGHT: The fall colors of maturing spirea against the sash of an old blue window. OPPOSITE, TOP LEFT: A spiral carved post is given a deep blue finish, creating the perfect contrast to the adobe wall behind. OPPOSITE, TOP CENTER: A detail of an old chair, long ago given a blue surface. OPPOSITE, TOP RIGHT: Contrasting blues highlight a glass-fronted door. OPPOSITE, BOTTOM LEFT: A bright blue entry gate offers privacy and welcomes. OPPOSITE, BOTTOM RIGHT: All the details on this patio are blue, and it looks out to the wild blue yonder.

Bedrooms

Bedrooms are intimate spaces, areas of refreshment and privacy. At any one time, they can be work areas, spas, or family rooms, but they should always be comfortable spaces to live in. Often our bedrooms seem almost monastic with their thick adobe walls and spare detailing. Of all places in the home, they are most likely to display a few great old textiles, particularly blankets and rugs with Navajo designs and serapes from old Mexico. In the past, people slept on adobe *bancos* covered with these textiles, which were then rolled up during the day so that rooms would convert back into living areas; few could afford the luxury of separate areas just for sleeping.

ABOVE RIGHT: Great old twin beds are placed foot to foot, creating a long seating area and guest quarters in this home on Canyon Road; Pendleton blankets serve as bedspreads.
RIGHT: A detail of a guest room, with *molas*— appliquéd shirt tops made by the Cuna Indian women of the San Blas Islands—being used as pillow tops and a New Mexican carved figure of the Virgin of Guadalupe.
OPPOSITE, TOP: An old metal-framed bed, with a wonderful black-patterned bed skirt and sham that contrast with a simple white bedspread, gives this room the feeling of an old Mexican hacienda. A shelf around the room holds vintage Mexican pottery.
OPPOSITE, BOTTOM: Bright red vintage Mexican serapes, once made for the tourist trade, are now highly collectible and make this guest room a lively spot.

OPPOSITE: Old beams, thick walls, and plain floors and surfaces bring a sense of timeless comfort to this bedroom. Even though the room is free of nonessentials, it remains warm and welcoming.
ABOVE: Filled with European antiques, a big bedroom is nonetheless clearly a Santa Fe room, with a charming fireplace and a beamed ceiling.

LEFT: A bed fills an alcove, and above the bed a long narrow *nicho* provides shelf space. ABOVE: Extra space is revealed in this pitched-roof home so that favorite old childhood toys and trunks find a space and the bed is given an alcovelike setting.

Baths

In addition to its obvious function, the bathroom in a desert climate is a sanctuary for the pleasurable uses of water. Since the air here is always dry and the day often warm or dusty, baths are a joy. Big old tubs or fancy new ones with swirls and jets will be hung with plants or will incorporate windows for gazing out onto the landscape. There are bound to be tile-covered walls and counters, thanks to the Spanish and Arab penchant for tiled surfaces that found a home in Santa Fe. Besides water, the bathroom can also be a place for fire. It is hard to imagine a more sensual experience of elements than enjoying a fire in a small corner fireplace while soaking in a bathtub, in a thick-walled adobe room, and gazing into the night sky through an open window.

ABOVE RIGHT: An intimate space given lots of detail, including the patterns formed by the pierced sconce shades. RIGHT: A detail of the sink from the bath above shows that the tile and sink were created for this warm little bathroom. OPPOSITE, TOP: No part of the house is neglected for displaying collections: This bath offers a collection of crosses and other Southwestern and Latin American art as well as a grazing spot for a few woolly Navajo goats. OPPOSITE, BOTTOM LEFT: Just above the water line in the shower, a collection of antique beaded bags. OPPOSITE, BOTTOM RIGHT: A skylight above beams light into this extraordinary bathroom which features small tiles from floor to ceiling, creating a very Moorish effect. By the basin, a ceramic figure from Atzompa, Mexico.

Tile

In Santa Fe, the decorative use of tiles is rarely restrained, whether in the bath or in other parts of the home. They become an avenue of expression on stairs, kitchen walls, and around fountains and pools. Wherever there is water, you are especially likely to find tiles. In New Mexico, the use of tiles seems to come from old Mexico, where a long history of manufacture continues to provide a vast array of designs from which to choose. As in Puebla, old Mexico's premier city of tile, with its decorated facades, there is a penchant here for the use of cobalt blue and soft cream, with splashes of other colors adding to geometric or organic designs. While the early New Mexican colonists might own one of the great pots or bowls produced in the Talavera potteries of old Mexico, there is no evidence for the actual importing of tile—lugging heavy earthenware tiles along the Camino Real's thousands of miles would have been unthinkable. But in some of the earliest structures—the mission churches—there is evidence of dados and other surfaces being painted to represent tiles, showing that the love of the ornamental surface ran very deep. And it finds resonance in the continued play of ornamental walls in our homes today.

PREVIOUS PAGES: Two bathrooms share an aesthetic of clean, plain design, allowing the architecture to dominate.

OPPOSITE: A painting by Diego Rivera of a Calla lily vendor serves as an inspiration for the tiled mural in this shower. RIGHT: By the second half of the twentieth century, imported tile from Mexico came to be a standard in most Santa Fe bathrooms, as seen in this backsplash in an older home. BELOW RIGHT: In a wonderful old garden, a vintage tile mural featuring an armorial crest enlivens the outdoor space. BELOW: A tile plaque, probably from Spain, of Don Quixote de la Mancha is overhung with vines in one corner of a garden.

Quiet Corners

As precious as our sleep is to us, we also value special places in our home that invite us to stop and rest. These spots are enhanced by simple objects and plants, and, most intangibly, by the pattern of light, giving us space for private thoughts.

ABOVE: One side of a bedroom opens to a small greenhouse-like area with just enough room for a few happy geraniums and a rocking chair. OPPOSITE, TOP LEFT: A portal on this home has been enclosed to form both an entry and a place to rest and read. OPPOSITE, BOTTOM LEFT: Geraniums at the window capture our attention for a few seconds and then allow us to go on with the day, refreshed. OPPOSITE, RIGHT: This little hideaway can serve as an occasional guest room; it invites tranquility, with its curtains and built-in bed.

Rincon de la Siesta

ABOVE: A panoramic view of La Quinta.
OPPOSITE, LEFT: Pioneer landscape architect
Rose Greeley came from Washington, D.C., in
the 1930s to design the original gardens, many
of which have been maintained. OPPOSITE, TOP
RIGHT: A wall tile honoring the house's patron
saint, San Isidro Labrador. OPPOSITE, BOTTOM
RIGHT: These wrought-iron gates represent the
finest craftsmanship available in New Mexico
when the house was constructed.

Los Poblanos y La Quinta

IN ALBUQUERQUE'S NORTH VALLEY, LOS POBLANOS WAS A SMALL AGRICULTURAL
VILLAGE SETTLED BY FAMILIES FROM PUEBLA, MEXICO, IN THE EIGHTEENTH
CENTURY. IN THE 1930S, THIS VILLAGE BECAME HOME TO ALBERT SIMMS AND
RUTH HANNA McCORMICK, A WIDOWER AND WIDOW WHO MET WHILE
SERVING IN THE U.S. CONGRESS. WITH THE HELP OF SANTA FE ARCHITECT
JOHN GAW MEEM, THEY CREATED A FARM ESTATE WHERE THEY COULD LIVE
AND ENTERTAIN. TODAY THE ESTATE SERVES AS A CULTURAL CENTER,
LA QUINTA, AND AS AN HISTORIC INN, LOS POBLANOS.

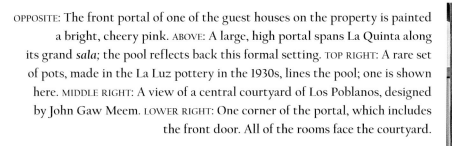

OPPOSITE: The front portal of one of the guest houses on the property is painted a bright, cheery pink. ABOVE: A large, high portal spans La Quinta along its grand *sala*; the pool reflects back this formal setting. TOP RIGHT: A rare set of pots, made in the La Luz pottery in the 1930s, lines the pool; one is shown here. MIDDLE RIGHT: A view of a central courtyard of Los Poblanos, designed by John Gaw Meem. LOWER RIGHT: One corner of the portal, which includes the front door. All of the rooms face the courtyard.

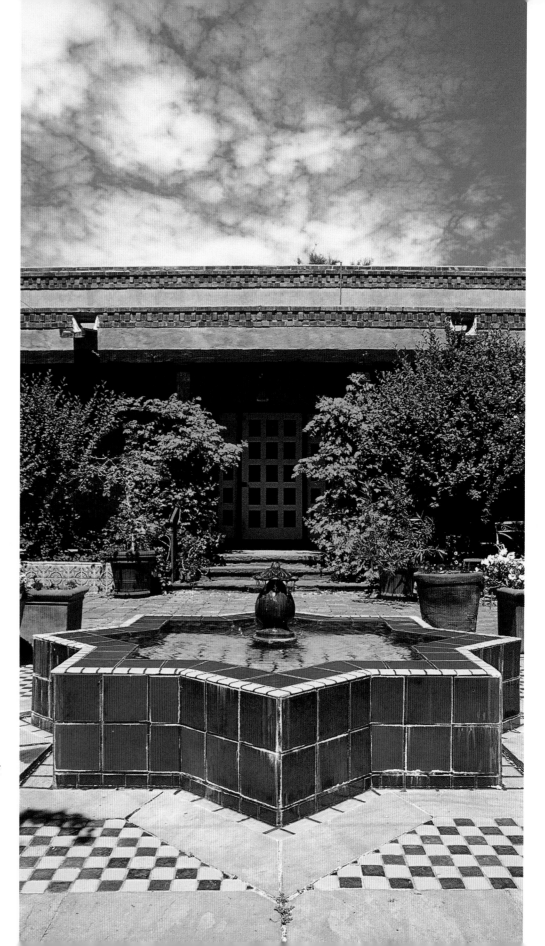

RIGHT: At the country inn, a star-shaped fountain greets visitors and provides a cool respite from the New Mexico sun; the surrounding portal also helps to moderate the intense light and heat. OPPOSITE: A view of the extraordinary bathing room at La Quinta, along with details of the wall painting, a folk masterpiece of decorative whimsy. This room was designed to serve the many guests at La Quinta who used the big formal pool.

Fountains and Pools

There is never enough water here, so we crave watery things: fountains and lush vegetation, flowing streams and deep pools. For the most part we cannot have them, so those lucky enough to have true pools of "live water" have many friends. While water is a blessing, it can also be a curse in a desert climate, since few homes were constructed to withstand any sort of flood. Dry riverbeds can become lethal in a downpour of torrential rain. Ironically, flooding is endemic, since sudden rains will rush right over the long-hardened, dry soil. Small cracks in our stucco walls and *canales*, or drainspouts, can invite instantaneous rivers and waterfalls for our flat roofs.

ABOVE LEFT: Flowering plants line this secluded pool. TOP RIGHT: A pool provides a long view to the Jemez Mountains. ABOVE RIGHT: Viewed from the protective portal, the pool at La Quinta sits amidst formal gardens.

RIGHT: Artist Sally Chandler has created an entire world within her garden with mosaic murals and fountains like this one. OPPOSITE: The blue basin of this fountain heightens the sense of coolness; in the distance, an entry gate and lots of flowering plants.

OPPOSITE: Bubbling or calm, the stone fountains found in Santa Fe courtyards provide an instant sense of tranquility. ABOVE: Hanging plants and an old central fountain at the Cassidy compound provide a hidden oasis.

Home Is Where the Heart Is

HIGH ON THE LIST OF THINGS TO DO IN SANTA FE IS A VISIT TO DOODLET'S, A STORE NEAR THE PLAZA THAT DEFIES A SIMPLE DESCRIPTION, FILLED AS IT IS WITH THE MAGICAL ACCUMULATION OF ONE PERSON'S QUIRKY OBSESSIONS AND CHERISHED OBJECTS. THE NATIVE SANTA FEAN WHO OWNS DOODLET'S HAS A HOME THAT SURPASSES THE STORE IN ITS DIVINE QUIRKINESS. A GATHERING OF TREASURES, HER HOUSE HOLDS ALL THOSE THINGS THAT SHE SIMPLY COULD NOT PART WITH; IT IS A PLACE FILLED WITH ALL THE COMPASSION AND WHIMSY OF ITS OWNER.

OPPOSITE: A deep portal can accommodate and protect furniture, including a bed for summer outdoor sleeping. LEFT: Salvaged fencing, old crosses, and Shasta daisies create an area of the garden. ABOVE: Irises are the spring flags of Santa Fe, waving from every garden.

BELOW: Crows, fish, crosses, and countless other pieces of folk and fun art crowd the house. From the living room, an old door from the early years of the twentieth century leads to a guest bedroom. RIGHT: The living room is filled with light, simple furniture and decorated with happy memories.

OPPOSITE, TOP LEFT: Small shelves hold smaller religious miniatures. OPPOSITE, TOP RIGHT: A group of folk *retablos* upon a chest. OPPOSITE, BOTTOM: Numerous reliquaries and votive figures decorate doors, tables, and specially designed *nichos*. BELOW: An extraordinary pantry off the kitchen is loaded with overflow collections.

OPPOSITE, TOP: Old shell-shaped tiles have been placed behind the sink. OPPOSITE, BOTTOM: A bedroom with thick walls and light pouring in from the back garden area; on the bed, a homemade quilt reflects the sentiments of its owner and creator. LEFT: Above the corner fireplace, more shrines and votive pieces. BELOW: The kitchen seen from two views is large and open, with plenty of room for gatherings and folk art.

Tinwork

The urge to add light in dark rooms and somber churches resulted in the development of decorative tinwork, one of New Mexico's most cherished folk arts. The use of tin for household items began in earnest during New Mexico's Territorial Period, when the materials needed—tin, glass, paint, wallpaper, chromolithographic prints, and tools—were first made available to local craftsmen, following the opening of the Old Santa Fe Trail to large-scale mercantile enterprises. Between 1850 and 1900 tin sconces, candleholders, mirrors, frames, boxes, crosses, *nichos*, and chandeliers appeared. Skilled Spanish and Native American craftsmen exploited the simple technology of cut-and-punched, painted-and-folded tin, creating myriad objects that offered not only utility but also bright, reflective surfaces for light. By the turn of the twentieth century, the interest in Mission style architecture throughout the Southwest fueled a revival in the use of tinwork for hotels, colleges, museums, and other large-scale public building projects in California, Arizona, and New Mexico. Workshops initiated by the WPA in New Mexico created a whole new generation of artisans. During the annual Spanish Market in Santa Fe, yet another generation of tinsmiths sell their craft to eager homeowners seeking to add a bit of light, color, and art to their houses just as homeowners throughout the centuries have done.

All of the frames, sconces, and *nichos* here show the same direct use of tin, with such decorative additions as reverse-painted glass, wallpaper, religious prints, and house paints.

Rooted in Tesuque

JANE SMITH'S HOME IN TESUQUE IS TUCKED
BACK ON ONE OF THE LITTLE TWISTING STREETS
THAT TYPIFY THIS RURAL VILLAGE ON THE
BANKS OF THE TESUQUE RIVER. OLD TREES,
ADOBE FARMHOUSES, AND GENTLY CURVING DIRT
ROADS PROVIDE A PASTORAL SETTING FOR HER
GARDEN COTTAGE, WHICH WAS DESIGNED TO
HARMONIZE IN SCALE AND AMBIANCE WITH ITS
ENVIRONS. INSIDE, THE HIGH PITCHED-ROOF
HOUSE IS REMINISCENT OF THE MOUNTAIN HOMES
OF NORTHERN NEW MEXICO AND PROVIDES
PLENTY OF LIGHT AND SPACE.

ABOVE: The living room contains many examples of religious art from colonial Latin America. Windows above act as skylights, and long formal windows give direct visual access to the gardens. LEFT: The dining area is next to the living room.

ABOVE: As ivy works its way up, windows with faded blue shutters give this home a tranquil country atmosphere. OPPOSITE, TOP: A quiet guest bedroom with headboards carved to resemble the carved-shell lunette so typical of New Mexican furniture and frames. OPPOSITE, BOTTOM: Small fences and low walls protect the house, including this section of the garden.

Windows

Our era favors big windows, framed vistas, broad views, and streams of light filling high, open rooms. There are plenty of views to frame and even more light to enjoy in New Mexico, blessed as we are with mountain and mesa views and regular sunshiny days. But time was when our windows were tiny, or even entirely absent, and light was an infrequent visitor to our small, low-ceilinged rooms. This was a true state of poverty, for it arose from a scarcity of building materials, a lack of heating, and, above all, a need for defense against invaders. Once these conditions receded, adobe homes came to include big paned windows. As if to make up for the centuries of hardship, New Mexicans embraced the opportunity to turn their windows into something special. Simple, effective moldings with pediments or whimsical curves and volutes emerged, and color was added to offset the plain, adobe-plastered walls. The repertoire of possible window styles continues, with each generation adding to the mix.

Cupboards

With little furniture, few possessions, and no closets, early New Mexican householders were able to keep track of their important goods in a few big chests and well-guarded cupboards. These cupboards, called *trasteros*, along with the large six-board chests that were used for hauling and storage, have become prized possessions of contemporary New Mexicans. Blessed with great regional art, Santa Feans will make cupboards a focal point in almost any room. Old New Mexican cupboards have become difficult if not impossible to obtain, so we scour shops and markets for great nineteenth- and early-twentieth-century examples from our neighbors to the south, east, and west. If we are lucky, we find cupboards in the same simple styles that typified the country pine pieces that were once the most important items of furniture in a New Mexican home or church.

OPPOSITE: Open for viewing, a big old Mexican cupboard is now home to a folk-art collection, primarily of Mexican ceramics. LEFT: A green kitchen cupboard, probably from Mexico, finds new life and great utility in a contemporary kitchen. ABOVE: An old blacksmith's cabinet found at a country antique market in Michigan now houses an abundance of miniature folk animals from the Mather collection. In front, a sheep made by late folk artist Felipe Archuleta guards the cupboard.

FAR LEFT: A small bathroom filled with pink, orange, and magenta. ABOVE LEFT: A rare spot of white, the fireplace blazes with votive candles; above it are stuffed fowl. The large female ceramic figure is from Ocotlan, Mexico. ABOVE: Colorful objects fill the shelves, adding to this riotous collection. LEFT: A crucifixion scene of carved and painted wood by Antonio Villafañe of Oaxaca, Mexico. OPPOSITE: Exuberant and eclectic, this living area explodes with color.

Behold the Many Colors

ALICE ANN BIGGERSTAFF COMES TO HER HOME IN SANTA FE WITH A DEEP LOVE OF THE LOCAL COLOR. A PROFESSIONAL COLORIST BEFORE THERE WAS SUCH A THING, SHE SPENT HER CAREER AT HALLMARK IN KANSAS CITY BUT ALWAYS MADE REGULAR VISITS TO SANTA FE. FINALLY SHE RETIRED HERE AND BEGAN TO CREATE A UNIQUE HAVEN IN HER FAVORITE TOWN. *AVID* HARDLY DESCRIBES THE ENTHUSIASM REVEALED IN HER COLLECTION OF FOLK ART. EACH DAY THERE IS A NEW PROJECT FOR ALICE ANN AS SHE MIXES AND STIRS COLORS AND TEXTURES AND CULTURES TOGETHER INTO A TRUE RAINBOW OF DELIGHT.

RIGHT: A row of bright serapes and vintage blankets. BELOW: Wild paper flowers adorn a pineapple pot from central Mexico. OPPOSITE, TOP LEFT: A carved-and-painted shrine from Mexico atop a pile of Latin American textiles. OPPOSITE, TOP RIGHT: A glimpse into a cupboard offers a riotous view of folk pottery from all over. OPPOSITE, BOTTOM LEFT: The cupboards and drawers are literally spilling over with textiles and folk art. OPPOSITE, BOTTOM RIGHT: A doll door with a Sacred Heart.

ABOVE LEFT AND LEFT: An entire home dedicated to a folk-art collection that is destined for eventual placement in a museum. Large *nichos* and broad *bancos* provide display areas for this collection, which focuses on the arts of Africa and Latin America. OPPOSITE: A skylight showcases a collection of Mexican masks. In the foreground a large Taos drum serves as a table.

Collecting Ethnic Arts

The creative enthusiasms of Santa Feans—
their quest to understand cultures other than
their own, their interest in living somewhat
outside mainstream culture among others
committed to a personal aesthetic—have led
our town to become the nation's center for
the folk arts. Through Santa Fe's renowned
Museum of International Folk Art and regular
markets dedicated to ethnic and folk arts,
along with galleries devoted to the same, we
find plenty of opportunities to explore various
cultures. Our homes are a reflection of these
interests; some could be staging areas for
future museum collections and exhibitions.
Many of the factors that originally drew non-
native New Mexicans to the community over a
century ago—the exotic nature of indigenous
cultures, the urge to escape Western civiliza-
tion, the energetic appeal of so-called "primitive" or folk art—continue to draw collectors.
And then there is the very nature of our adobe
homes, raw and vibrant, primitive and utilitarian. Our history as Mexico's frontier has
played a role in our passion for the arts of other
cultures. Whatever our personal background
may be, we live with a comfortable mix of
expression—Continental antiques and Peru-
vian textiles, country furniture and wooden
pigs, African sculpture and Saltillo tiles—
finding that there is room in our homes for an
alliance of all things strange and beautiful.

ABOVE: A group of Mexican masks hang from a butcher's table from Mexico. ABOVE CENTER: Dance wands from southern Mexico hang in a stairwell. ABOVE RIGHT: Animals by the late folk artist Felipe Archuleta at the Mathers' home. FAR RIGHT: This corner fireplace is covered with slingshots made by the Cuna Indians of Panama. CENTER RIGHT: A beaded crown from Africa. RIGHT: A group of crows and other birds by the late Navajo folk artist Woody Herbert.

AIR

The colors are vivid pink with fresh green; the season
is summer; and the place to be is outside in the courtyards,
which are full of sunshine and flowers.

Santa Fe is up in the air, at times in the clouds, close to the stars and sun, and always a bit of an ephemeral city—it is airy. In summer, the sweet dryness of the atmosphere makes the climate, even on days when the temperature starts to climb, nothing short of ideal. In winter, the same dryness gives an added crispness and bite to the clear days. The winds sweep the clouds into crazy cigar shapes over the mountains for weeks on end in fall, while in the summer stately pink-tinged cumulus clouds ride the aerial currents. We can watch the weather coming and going, gaze at the purple-hazed mountains far to the west, study the scuttling, low-hanging gray clouds of water and snow, and awake to streaks of pink and orange across the eastern sky. Broad vistas are up and out, and all around. The sky seems big. There are the clouds to watch, the sunsets and sunrises to contemplate, the weather to consider, and the scents to sample—a breath of Santa Fe air is high and dry.

Santa Fe in the summer is full, busy, and fun. Suddenly the town becomes a mecca for those who seek art and culture along with an ideal physical setting of sunny days and cool nights. For the locals there is the dual-edged sword of relishing the bustling excitement with the more difficult task of sharing our streets and sidewalks, guest rooms, and parking spaces with visitors. Some retreat to their homes and gardens for the duration, avoiding the activity of the city center, happy to find their entertainment in more solitary pleasures. For them, the focus upon nurturing new life can provide plenty of challenges.

A solid ramada looks out to the soft but spectacular foothills of the Sangre de Cristo Mountains, providing plenty of shaded space for sitting on the built-in *bancos* that are covered with vividly colored Mexican serapes.

OPPOSITE, CLOCKWISE FROM TOP LEFT: A garden dream bed in Chimayo. A handful of Santa Fe's flowers adorn a bright blue bench that sits against a front porch wall painted to match. A poppy in vivid pink. Along Gypsy Alley, mailboxes bloom like summer flowers. ABOVE: The far horizon of the mountains, with geraniums in the foreground. FAR RIGHT: Bright cosmos—a portrait of perfection. RIGHT: The wonderful pink-purple lilacs of the early summer against a garden gate.

SUMMER

If the rain gods are willing, we garden. It is a toss-up how we garden—with water or without it. We can plant drought-resistant native plants, or we can go with old thirsty favorites. Mostly, though, we do a bit of both. This politic way of gardening suits our needs, since we have learned that the wild, open spaces of the great Southwest can be tamed only with careful planning. We try to integrate walls, buildings, trees, and plants to bring the open landscape under control and provide intimate spaces for living in our high-desert climate. Enclosed courtyards and walled yards create finite gardens that spill out onto tiny plots of grass. Old trees along streets and drives bring coolness, shade, and elegance to the streetscape.

As summer settles in, we are likely to plant almost anything if we think it might grow. If we guess wrong, our experiments quickly become crisped, so there is a tendency to rely on perennial favorites that don't need much babying, along with a handful of natives that are often a bit weedy. Sometimes we turn to pots of geraniums, since these have such a reliable local reputation. But geraniums need our attention and water, water, water. Hoses, drip systems, buckets, sprays, soaker hoses, sprinklers, watering cans—all are employed as we watch our water bills climb to new heights. And then comes the guilt: We know that our enthusiasm for full gardens has overcome our intentions to be environmentally prudent and thoughtful. High-desert gardening remains our most constant oxymoron.

An exuberant kitchen garden
sheltered by high walls.

Sitting Out

From May through October, it is possible to move life from inside to outdoors in Santa Fe, and this is exactly what we do. Unlike its neighbor to the south, the Sonoran desert with which our terrain is too frequently confused, the high-desert landscape of Santa Fe rarely reaches unbearably hot temperatures. With cool nights and a dryness that discourages biting insects, the air becomes like a second skin, allowing us to spend hours outside. Walls, flowers, vines, coyote fences, lattice, awnings, umbrellas, trees, portals, patios, and porches—all define outdoor living areas where old furniture can be placed for resting after the rigors of barbecuing, gardening, or Frisbee. From here we can talk through the day, watch the sunset play upon the broad skies in the evening, and see the moonrise cast its shadows against the blue-white ground at night. Late August finds us flat on our backs on car hoods, lawns, hammocks, and couches, trying to spot each of the thousands of meteors streaking across the sky.

In our outdoor rooms we are free from screens and windows, and open to the sky, yet we bring much of the design sensibility of real rooms to our fantastic little outside spaces. Many of these garden areas are true extensions of the home, sharing with it the creativity that is so much a part of life in Santa Fe. Here we can be even freer with our visual puns and splashy colors. To this open living room, we often add water to soothe us and shade to moderate the searing directness of the sun.

TOP LEFT: A whimsical seating area is created by this turquoise-painted lattice, potted plants, and various examples of garden art. ABOVE: A chair amid a riot of petunias and other flowering plants. LEFT: An entire outdoor living space, with an area for cooking, a fireplace, and a seating area. Climbing plants contrast with crisp black-and-white stripes in this cool setting. FAR LEFT: An arborlike setting is created with lashed poles, resulting in a living area in the garden surrounded by hollyhocks.

Dining Out

The protected spaces created by courtyards, high walls, and deep portals have become important for living, working, and dining out. There is no better place to watch the evening unfold than within the confines of the courtyard, with the fountain playing in the background. Since the weather is so congenial during the summer and fall, even those without a courtyard can define an outdoor dining space that might include a broad vista or garden setting.

The courtyard has an ancient heritage in both the New and Old Worlds; it is an architectural creation of universal appeal. The plaza among the Pueblo Indians functioned in much the same manner as the central open space of the Spanish village. Open, it was also protected and could be sealed off from unwanted intrusion. Inside, communal social activities could be safely conducted. The courtyard of the Spanish home functioned in much the same way. Anglo newcomers to the West found the arrangement very much to their liking, and it was quickly added to their architectural repertoire. Today we still work and play within our protected courtyards and plazas, enjoying the benefits of a space open to nature, but comfortably secure and private.

LEFT: A most dramatic hilltop is made manageable by a low wall and some high-desert plantings. The ring of the mountains beyond is echoed in the shape of the patio.
TOP RIGHT: A wonderfully eclectic grouping of garden objects fills a well-shaded courtyard.
CENTER AND BOTTOM RIGHT: Simple chairs and plain tables along with a bit of shade are almost all it takes to create a quiet haven, once the landscape is walled and safe from the winds and intruders.

OPPOSITE: A deep portal and a big outdoor fireplace with seating offer the perfect ambience for enjoying a summer evening. The house and the back wall provide a protected courtyard setting. ABOVE: Extraordinary beams and corbels create a wonderful setting. Once the home of Santa Fe artist Gerald Cassidy and writer Ina Sizer Cassidy, it has been the setting for countless summer gatherings.

Garden Gates

Among the most charming elements of any home, a gate is the nature lover's preferred entryway to a garden, indicating the magic that lies within. New Mexicans are fond of simple, handmade structures, massive imposing ones, and everything in between. Each is appreciated for its individualism, and most take on a hearty patina under the fierce sun.

Almost as important to us as our doors or entry gates, our garden gates come in many designs, befitting from the large repertoires of the early Hispanic woodworkers, Native American carpenters, Mexican and Spanish ornamental ironworkers, and other craftsmen who have contributed to Santa Fe's visual vocabulary. Neglecting no opportunity for creative expression, Santa Feans also fashion their own idiosyncratic gates.

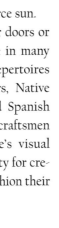

OPPOSITE, TOP LEFT: Coyote fencing deters varmints and creates a wonderful setting for a garden and garden gate. OPPOSITE, TOP CENTER: Great staffs of hollyhocks greet the visitor. The high adobe wall and gate provide no clue to what might lay beyond, yet they are far from formidable elements in this streetscape setting. OPPOSITE, TOP RIGHT: Beautiful ironwork on a filigreed gate leads to equally elegant gardens beyond. OPPOSITE, BOTTOM: While these large gates seem imposing, they provide a transition between the area outside the wall and the entry courtyard. Great slabs of flagstone and a wonderful, funky wheelbarrow full of petunias are part of this grand entrance. ABOVE: Old wood, a mysterious carved plaque, a rugged stone wall, and, beyond, a garden brimming with flowering plants provide the type of outdoor tableau that is ideal for the setting and climate.

OPPOSITE LEFT: Santa Feans love the old gates of Mexico, given a new life here. OPPOSITE, TOP RIGHT: Adobe buttresses set this gate apart. OPPOSITE, BOTTOM RIGHT: The intense blue of this gate, with its dark frame and corbels, makes it a standout. ABOVE: Shadows created by the strong Southwestern sun and protruding beams give this wall special drama.

Santa Fe Flowers

Our favorite plants can be found along the river and acequia, and in old neighborhoods. Early spring lilacs and flashy poppies are often out of control, as are the ever rambunctious but lovable Castilian roses—so briefly do these local rose favorites appear that we tend to forget about them until they flash their yellow or orange faces amid a tangle of green. Along with bedding plants, bushes, and bulbs, we adore the brilliant blooms of our fruit trees and mourn the loss of their blossoms in our frequent hard freezes. There are numerous garden clubs and societies here, each with its faithful nurturing a prized iris or rose, selling plants on the Plaza, or providing tours to spectacular gardens. In spite of water shortages and high water bills, we all try to add color to life in this high-desert environment. Xeriscape gardening, that is, gardens adapted to a dry environment, must be part of each gardener's consideration, but still we can't resist the old favorites.

OPPOSITE: Bright red roses against an adobe wall. CLOCKWISE, FROM LEFT: Despite the high altitude and snowy winters, Santa Fe has its share of cacti, including these brilliant chollas. Poppies and yarrow are hardy perennials much favored in our gardens. When and if it blooms, there is nothing quite as elegant as the ancient wisteria that wind across walls and portals.

Portals

The portal is so essential to the architecture of Santa Fe that we take its importance for granted. The word *portal* has quietly entered the local vocabulary, becoming "spanglicized" in its plural form to *portals* rather than the correct *portales*. Throughout Latin America, in tropical towns with blazing sun and heavy rains, plaza areas are ringed by buildings with deep portals—porches that traverse the entire length of the buildings—so that pedestrians can be protected from mud, rain, and sun. Santa Fe's most famous is the grand portal of the Palace of the Governors, where Native Americans sell their wares outside throughout the year. It is now possible to walk almost entirely around the Plaza and be protected by portals, with only quick dashes through open spaces. Similarly, homes with central patios or buildings with an interior *placita*, a little plaza, often offer small-scale examples of this fundamental arrangement.

Portals are not found only at the front of a home, but can also run across the entire length of the back of the house. Old homes that were built by accretion—one room at a time added until a courtyard was formed—often had no hallways or interior doors so that movement from room to room was accomplished entirely by walking under the portal. Portals are work spaces, sitting areas, dining rooms, garden spots, hallways, and walkways all rolled into one.

OPPOSITE: A long, broad portal offers shade and protection to the home and becomes an important living area. LEFT: Many portals are given a coat of white paint so that reflected light will fill the shaded space. BELOW: These portals wrap around more than one side of the house, acting both as entry porches and as ample living areas.

Each of these portals demonstrates how the length, breadth, and design of these structures add character and utilitarian beauty to homes. There are many simple variations on the design of the portal but its basic outline of posts and beams makes it a paragon of simplicity and practicality.

Pots in the Garden

Pots full of plants often take the place of big flower gardens in Santa Fe since they provide a mutable and mobile source of color. The garden is the perfect place to indulge our fascination in the shape, texture, and color of thick, sturdy pottery. Old jars once used for transporting oil and wine throughout the world find a place of rest in Santa Fe portals while bulbous *ollas*, or water jars, made by the Tarahumara Indians of northern Mexico travel north from native villages to the famed Santa Fe flea market. Geraniums are the hands-down favorites among the potted plants of Santa Fe. They can be wintered by a sunny window and set out again when the weather allows.

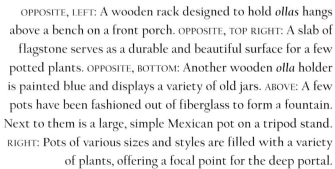

OPPOSITE, LEFT: A wooden rack designed to hold *ollas* hangs above a bench on a front porch. OPPOSITE, TOP RIGHT: A slab of flagstone serves as a durable and beautiful surface for a few potted plants. OPPOSITE, BOTTOM: Another wooden *olla* holder is painted blue and displays a variety of old jars. ABOVE: A few pots have been fashioned out of fiberglass to form a fountain. Next to them is a large, simple Mexican pot on a tripod stand. RIGHT: Pots of various sizes and styles are filled with a variety of plants, offering a focal point for the deep portal.

ABOVE: A small shrine set directly into the garden wall. ABOVE RIGHT: An adobe-style birdhouse for a winged Santa Fean. RIGHT: A beautiful wrought-iron cross set in the garden with a foreground of nasturtiums.

Collecting Garden Art

There are many visual delights in a garden, not all of them having to do with living things. Gardens can offer up a spot of beauty, whimsy, or happenstance amid the glory of blooming plants and flowers. The art of the garden might be a small shrine that fades and chips into a state of perfection, or an old watering can toted for generations until its battered sides take on the heavy patina of well-used tools. Sometimes it is the chance intersection of flowers at their moment of glory with a garden gate's pattern or the light filtering down through the trees to a flaking bench set with a gardener's snack of iced tea and crackers. These moments—little visual epiphanies of light and color—can be brought on by the thoughtful placement of plants and playful or useful objects. The fact that this art is created only for a moment's pleasure—appearing without guarantee of reward—makes it all the more sweet and ever so slightly sad. In a community abounding with creative spirits, such delights exist around every corner.

ABOVE LEFT: A venerable watering can crosses over from the world of utility to that of art. LEFT: This little birdhouse was created with as much thought and art as the house where it hangs. RIGHT: It seems that the simplest transformations can be the most humorous and satisfying.

OPPOSITE: Garden art abounds, from a simple homemade shrine for St. Francis to old tin pots. Ceramic birds adorn a hanging pot, while live hummingbirds visit many a Santa Fe garden.
LEFT AND BELOW: The conjunction of blooms, walls, and a few carefully placed objects creates moments of visual delight.

Santa Fe's Monet

DOUG ATWILL'S HOME ON A TINY LANE JUST OFF CANYON ROAD IS PROOF THAT THE SPIRIT OF MONET CAN BE FOUND IN SANTA FE AS WELL AS IN GIVERNY. THE CAREFULLY CONCEIVED AND EXECUTED GARDENS THAT SURROUND HIS HOUSE ARE INTEGRATED NOT ONLY INTO HIS LIFE BUT ALSO INTO HIS ART, SERVING AS SUBJECTS FOR HIS PAINTING. KNOWN AS A BUILDER, RENOVATOR, AND DESIGNER, ATWILL FAVORS CLASSIC PROPORTIONS; SIMPLE, STRAIGHTFORWARD LAYOUTS; AND THE USE OF DETAILS INSPIRED BY TERRITORIAL-STYLE DWELLINGS. LARGE DOUBLE-HUNG WINDOWS, WHITE-PAINTED TRIM, AND BIG SHUTTERS ARE FURTHER SIGNATURES OF HIS STYLE. OVER THE YEARS, HE HAS TAKEN ON MANY PROJECTS AND HAS BROUGHT BACK TO LIFE A FEW OF SANTA FE'S FAVORITE HOMES. HIS IMPACT ON ARCHITECTURE AND DESIGN IN SANTA FE HAS BEEN IMMENSE, BUT HE CHOOSES TO WORK QUIETLY ON PROJECTS, FOCUSING ON BRINGING LANDSCAPE AND HOME INTO HARMONY.

OPPOSITE: A doorway is used to frame the garden beyond. LEFT: Not so carefully trained roses exuberantly cover the arch over a door that leads from the garden to the house. Doorways, windows, and arches are placed throughout the home and garden to capture views within the enclosed areas. BELOW: A broad bricked walkway and portal have the same simple but formal feel as the facade of the home. Bright white trim lends the perfect accent against the thick brown adobe walls.

ABOVE: A series of walls in the garden provides a path that is anything but direct. The big pot and wild blooming plant break up any sense of formality and reflect the good humor of the owner. OPPOSITE: The living room is opened wide to the outdoors by a wall of windows. The freshness of the room is further enhanced by the soft pink glow of the plaster walls. On one wall, Atwill's painting captures his garden forever.

RIGHT: A deep portal is used for summertime dining. BELOW: Plain cedar posts are used to define areas of the garden. OPPOSITE: Details of the Atwill garden, and a work in progress—a painting whose origins are made obvious by the views of the garden.

RIGHT AND OPPOSITE: Double doors open onto a broad front hallway that leads directly to the back of the house and the garden beyond. Common in large old adobe homes, this layout allows easy access to the garden and reflects an earlier time when carts and animals would go straight through the large front gates to the courtyard. Nowadays the arrangement serves to separate living areas, as well as to provide passage and a grand entranceway.

A Joy-Filled Home Along the Acequia

JOY AND BERNIE BUSCH WERE ABLE TO PREVAIL UPON THEIR FRIEND DOUG ATWILL TO DESIGN THEIR HOME ON A SMALL BUT
ROMANTIC LOT UNDER THE TREES THAT LINE THE ACEQUIA, THE ORIGINAL IRRIGATION DITCH FOR THE CITY. USING ALL THE
AVAILABLE SPACE, HE HELPED THEM CREATE A LITTLE HOME WITH A BIG HEART, HIGH CEILINGS, AND WONDERFUL ACCESS TO
BOTH THE STREET AND THE NARROW BACK GARDEN.

ABOVE: A plastered center fireplace is flanked by skylights, making the living room a light, airy space. LEFT: Living space on the portal was part of the original plan. French doors open directly off the living room. The corner fireplace provides warmth and cheer on cool evenings. OPPOSITE, LEFT: The big country kitchen has its dining area and fireplace located at the back of the house so that diners can look directly onto the garden. OPPOSITE RIGHT: Candles and flowers decorate the mantel.

A Village Farmhouse TAKING THE ROADS NORTH OF SANTA FE CAN LEAD YOU TO A NUMBER OF SMALL VILLAGES THAT, NOT LONG AGO, WERE ISOLATED FROM THE "BIG" TOWN. HERE, MODEST, FUNCTIONAL HOMES WERE BUILT TO LAST GENERATIONS, WITH GARDENS AND ORCHARDS SUPPLYING FOOD. WHILE MUCH OF THIS RURAL LIFE HAS VANISHED, THIS FORMER FARMHOUSE WITH PRODUCTIVE ORCHARDS STILL RETAINS ITS PASTORAL COMFORTS. THE OWNERS HAVE WORKED HARD TO PRESERVE THE CHARM OF THEIR COUNTRY HOME WHILE UPDATING IT FOR MODERN LIFE. THE GREATEST TRANSFORMATION OCCURS IN THE ADDITION OF A DEEP PORTAL ACROSS THE BACK OF THE HOUSE, WHICH PROVIDES A GRAND VISTA AND INTIMATE VIEWS OF THE ORCHARDS AND ACEQUIA BELOW.

OPPOSITE: A big side garden provides space for flowering plants and a bit of lawn. LEFT: A gate and steps create a more formal entryway to the home. BELOW: The front-door entryway leads directly to the portal beyond. The skylight provides plenty of light for the art and plants of the entryway.

ABOVE: A big *trastero* on the porch provides a hiding place for tools. The deep red of the dado contrasts with the crisp white wood-work of the porch railings. The "pots" are punched tin in the New Mexican tradition.
LEFT: The porch is a viewing and seating area as well as a walkway around the house. Stairs off the porch lead to the orchard below.

Even as the sun sets, the ramada
emphasizes the contrast between sky
and earth, sun and shadow.

Ramadas

Like a room open to the sky, the ramada frames the landscape beyond and focuses the garden while also providing much needed shade. Deriving from the Spanish word *rama*, or branches, ramadas were originally built out of wood and scrub to provide temporary shade for cattle; they were also quickly built shelters for pioneer folks. Today, they maintain their folksy origins as easily built structures that offer shade without the formality and foundations of buildings and porches.

THE SANTA FE DIRECTORY

I. HOME ELEMENTS

BASICS

ADOBE AND CONSTRUCTION

Accent Adobe
P.O. Box 30801
Albuquerque, NM 87190
505-884-8493
Adobe subcontractor.

Adobe Factory
P.O. Box 219
Alcalde, NM 87511
505-852-4131
Traditional adobe manufacturer.

Living Structures
1594 San Mateo Lane
Santa Fe, NM 87505
505-988-2202
Healthy energy-efficient homes.
Alternative wall systems. Green building,
straw bale, pumicecrete.

Rio Abajo Adobe Works
7 Industrial Park Lane
Belen, NM 87004
505-864-6191
Makers of adobe bricks.

Woods Architects-Builders
302 Catron Street
Santa Fe, NM 87501
505-988-2413
Coauthor Sharon Woods has led this firm
in designing, building, and remodeling
Santa Fe's custom homes for more than
twenty-five years.

FIREPLACES AND FIREWOOD

A-1 Firewood
3134 Bridge Boulevard SW
Albuquerque, NM 87121
505-242-8181
Delivery available, full and half cords.

Casey's Top Hat Chimney Sweeps
7921 Old Santa Fe Trail
Santa Fe, NM 87501
505-989-5775
Fireplace cleaning.

The Firebird
1808 Espinacitas
Santa Fe, NM 87505
505-983-5264
Wood-burning, gas, and pellet stoves.

Firewood Company of Santa Fe
Rowe, NM
505-757-8555
Firewood delivered, or may be picked up.

Rios Wood and Freight Service
324 Camino del Monte Sol
Santa Fe, NM 87501
505-982-0358
Firewood, chips, bark, vigas, latillas, split
cedar.

LANDSCAPING

Cassidy's Landscaping
3901 Agua Fria
Santa Fe, NM 87501
505-474-4500
Landscape architects; installation,
consultation, and maintenance.

Chamisa Landscaping
129 Solana Drive
Santa Fe, NM 87501
505-988-3669
Custom design, installation, and
maintenance.

Design Workshop
506 Agua Fria
Santa Fe, NM 87501
505-982-8399
Licensed landscape architecture and site
planning.

Exterior Environments
P.O. Box 8197
Santa Fe, NM 87504
505-984-9969
Water-conscious and ecologically aware
landscapers.

The Green Edge, Inc.
1592 San Mateo Lane
Santa Fe, NM 87505
505-982-8257
A full-service landscape design and
construction company. Fountains, lighting,
stonework, erosion control, and waterfalls.

Edith Katz
24 Canada Village
Santa Fe, NM 87501
505-983-9207
Landscape architect and site planner.

Nature's Creations
4033 Cerrillos Road B-3
Santa Fe, NM 87505
505-471-2600
Ponds, reflecting pools, and waterfall
creations.

Southwest Fountains and Supply
6535 Edith Boulevard NE
Albuquerque, NM 87107
505-342-1150
Hand-carved stone fountains.

Stone Forest
213 S. St. Francis Drive
Santa Fe, NM 87501
505-986-8883
Hand-carved granite fountains and garden
ornaments.

Ulibarri Landscaping Materials
2805 Agua Fria Street
Santa Fe, NM 87507
505-471-7661
Full loads of fill dirt, topsoil, red cinders, and general landscaping material.

Wild Birds Unlimited
518 W. Cordova Road
Santa Fe, NM 87501
505-989-8818
Tabletop and outdoor fountains, birdbaths, accessories, and wild-bird seed.

Wilder Landscaping, Inc.
Richard Wilder
P.O. Box 5593
Santa Fe, NM 87502
505-989-8524
Landscape design, installation, and maintenance.

STONEWORK

Milestone, Inc.
1000 Cordova Place
Santa Fe, NM 87501
505-989-1999
Supplier of flagstone, moss rock, and veneer in addition to imported dimensional stone, tiles, and slabs from around the world.

Rocky Mountain Stone Company, Inc.
4741 Pan American Freeway NE
Albuquerque, NM 87197
505-345-8518
Large selection of marble, granite, slate, travertine, and natural stone.

Santa Fe Stone
901 W. San Mateo Road
Santa Fe, NM 87505
505-989-9514
Complete selection of exterior stone for landscaping, fountains, and more. All types of interior stone for flooring, countertops, sinks, fireplaces, and surrounds.

WALL PAINTING

All New Painting
Jody Feyas
1415 W. Alameda Suite E
Santa Fe, NM 87501
505-984-5022
Custom painting contractor; specialty finishes.

Ancient City Painting Co.
3039 Cliff Palace
Santa Fe, NM 87501
505-471-2556
Premium custom painting.

Guy's Painting
33 Bisbee Court, Suite E
Santa Fe, NM 87505
505-473-0093
Quality interior and exterior painting.

Old Paint Faux Finishes
505-986-3431
Specializing in reproducing textures in stone, wood, clay, and plaster.

Santa Faux Design
505-984-1790
Faux finishes.

WOOD PRODUCTS

Alpine Building Supply
493 W. Water Street
Santa Fe, NM 87501
505-982-2543
Upper grades of hardwoods and select softwoods, millwork, and hardwood flooring.

Frontier Wood
4523 State Road 14, Suite D
Santa Fe, NM 87505
505-474-9663
Reclaimed lumber; antique vigas, hand-hewn beams, ceiling decking, and flooring.

Hansen Lumber Company
1113 Calle Largo
Santa Fe, NM 87501
505-983-2774
Timbers, beams, vigas, latillas, posts, split cedar, salt cedar; lumber cut to specifications.

Lynch Fence Company
1545 Upper Canyon Road
Santa Fe, NM 87501
505-982-4076
Coyote fences sold and installed.

Norton Hill Wood Co., Inc.
701 Airport Road
Santa Fe, NM 87501
505-471-2456
Beams, vigas, cedar posts, and latillas.

Rios Excavating and Wrecking
1851 Rodeo Road
Santa Fe, NM 87505
505-471-7772
Recycled materials; lumber and vigas, brick, doors, and windows.

WOODWORKING

Armijo Design
420 Camino Don Miguel
Santa Fe, NM 87501
505-983-6050
Custom doors, furniture, and cabinetry.

Tony Barela
2010 Agua Fria, #E
Santa Fe, NM 87501
505-471-2609
Custom cabinetry and woodwork.

Robert Pepper Cabinetmaker
2878 Trades West Road
Santa Fe, NM 87504
505-471-0500
Contemporary and Southwest cabinetry.

Pittman Brothers Woodworks
1241 Siler Road
505-473-1199
Santa Fe, NM 87505
Modular kitchen and bath cabinets.

Samora's Woodworks
2873 Trades West Road
Santa Fe, NM 87504
505-471-5728
Custom architectural woodwork specializing in Santa Fe styles.

Wolfswinkel Enterprises
30 Oliver Court
Santa Fe, NM 87501
505-473-2058
Custom cabinetry and millwork.

DECORATIVE DETAILS

ANTIQUE DOORS

Antique Warehouse
530 S. Guadalupe Street, Suite B
Santa Fe, NM 87501
505-984-1159
Mexican doors, gates, and windows.

El Paso Imports
418 Cerrillos Road
Santa Fe, NM 87501
505-982-5698
Old Mexican doors, furniture, windows, gates, and reproductions.

La Compania Antigua Door Co.
2894 Trades West Road
Santa Fe, NM 87504
505-471-2971
Makers of fine furniture and doors.

Santa Fe Heritage
418 Montezuma Street
Santa Fe, NM 87501
505-983-5986
Re-creating the look of antiquity in door styles; specialty textures and authentic reproductions.

Spanish Pueblo Doors
1091 Siler Road, Unit B-1
Santa Fe, NM 87504
505-473-0464
Crafters of Southwest and country-style doors for more than four decades.

HARDWARE AND IRONWORK

Allbright & Lockwood Ltd.
621 Old Santa Fe Trail, Suite 5
Santa Fe, NM 87501
505-986-1715
European hardware, hand-forged cabinet hardware, and bathroom accessories.

Architectural Ironworks
2815 Industrial Road
Santa Fe, NM 87501
505-438-1864
A complete line of hand-cast door and cabinet hardware.

Christopher Thomson Ironworks
P.O. Box 578
Ribera, NM 87560
800-726-0145
Hand-forged steel furnishings, sculpture, and architectural works.

Custom Hardware
947 W. Alameda
Santa Fe, NM 87501
505-984-0879
Hardware, bathroom fixtures, and accessories to fit your every need.

Harmony Forge
800 Camino Consuelo
Santa Fe, NM 87505
505-471-3745
Distinctive ironwork.

Leonard's Ornamental Iron
02 Camino Charro
Santa Fe, NM 87501
505-471-6693
Custom interior and exterior railings, gates, and blacksmithing.

The Man of Steel
24 Las Estrellas
Santa Fe, NM 87505
505-473-7825
Custom fireplace screens, welding and fabrication.

Mesa Steel
4523 State Road 14, Suite D
Santa Fe, NM 87505
505-474-6811
Residential custom railings, gates, stairs, and ornamental iron.

Old World Hardware
621 Old Santa Fe Trail
Santa Fe, NM 87501
505-653-3566
Hand-forged hardware and lighting accessories.

LIGHTING

Artesanos Imports, Inc.
222 Galisteo Street
Santa Fe, NM 87501
505-983-1743
Imported Mexican lighting; wall sconces and chandeliers in a variety of metal finishes.

Latigo Lights
1208-A Parkway
Santa Fe, NM 87505
505-473-5836
Complete line of copper, tin, brass, and stainless steel fixtures; featuring Western, contemporary, and Southwest styles.

Native American Lighting Corporation
1911-D Riverside Drive
San Juan Pueblo, NM 87566
800-275-4113
Native American–owned company; large selection of audio and home entertainment theater lighting.

Palace Design
217 E. Palace Avenue
Santa Fe, NM 87501
505-988-5204
Distinctive designs, fine copper lamps and shades, wrought-iron lighting fixtures.

Southwestern Light
Rebecca Parsons
P.O. Box 548
Santa Fe, NM 87504
505-473-1077
The original Santa Fe–style hand-thrown pottery light fixtures. Ceiling-mounted lanterns and clusters, wagon-wheel chandeliers, wall mounts, and table lamps.

TILE

Arius Tile
114 Don Gaspar Avenue
Santa Fe, NM 87501
505-988-1196
Creator of handcrafted art tiles and murals.

Artesanos Imports, Inc.
222 Galisteo Street
Santa Fe, NM 87501
505-983-1743
Imported floor and wall tiles.

Casa Talavera
621 Rio Grande Boulevard NW
Albuquerque, NM 87104
505-243-2413
Authentic handmade Mexican tiles.

Counterpoint Tile
320 Sandoval Street
Santa Fe, NM 87504
505-982-1247
Represents several New Mexico artists and imports tiles from all over the world; floors, countertops, and fireplaces.

Saltillo Tile Company
851 W. San Mateo Road #4
Santa Fe, NM 87501
505-820-1830
Hand-painted Mexican talavera and Saltillo tile.

Statements in Tile
1440 Paseo de Peralta
Santa Fe, NM 87501
505-988-4440
Unusual tiles, with personal service.

TINWORK

Richard Fisher Tinworks
9 Griego Road
Tesuque, NM 87574
505-989-4227
Hand-stamped Northern New Mexico tinwork.

Fred Ray Lopez, Tinwork Gallery & Studio
227 Don Gaspar Avenue
Santa Fe, NM 87501
505-984-2922
Traditional New Mexican tinwork; chandeliers, candleholders, and mirrors.

ANTIQUES

Antiques on Grant
136 Grant Avenue
Santa Fe, NM 87501
505-995-9701
Eight dealers featuring furniture, textiles, folk art, and architectural items.

Mary Corley Antiques
215 N. Guadalupe Street
Santa Fe, NM 87501
505-984-0863
Country antiques and accessories from France, Spain, Italy, and England. Dried flower arrangements from the floral studio.

Foxglove Antiques
260 Hyde Park Road
Santa Fe, NM 87501
505-986-8285
*European country furniture; architectural
and garden elements.*

Ann Lawrence Antiques
805 Early Street, Suite D
Santa Fe, NM 87501
505-982-1755
*An eclectic resource for antique and vintage
European, tribal, and ethnic textiles.*

Tarman Galleries Ltd.
343 W. Manhattan Avenue
Santa Fe, NM 87501
505-983-2336
*Seventeenth- to nineteenth-century
American, Oriental, and European
furniture, porcelain, silver, etc.*

ART GALLERIES

Alan Houser, Inc.
P.O. Box 217
Santa Fe, NM 87502
505-471-1528
*Representing the estate of the renowned
Native American artist. By appointment
only.*

Allene Lapides Gallery
558 Canyon Road
Santa Fe, NM 87501
505-984-0191
*Regular gallery artists include Joe Andoe,
Marica Myers, James Havard, and Herb
Ritts.*

Andrea Fisher—Fine Pottery
221 W. San Francisco Street
Santa Fe, NM 87501
505-986-1234
*Native American pottery, primarily from
the Southwest.*

Andrew Smith Gallery
203 W. San Francisco Street
Santa Fe, NM 87501
505-984-1234
Classic and contemporary photography.

Bellas Artes Ltd.
653 Canyon Road
Santa Fe, NM 87501
505-983-2745
*Contemporary paintings, drawings, clay,
fiber, African and pre-Columbian art.*

Canfield Gallery
414 Canyon Road
Santa Fe, NM 87501
505-988-4199
*Modernist paintings of the twentieth
century, as well as antique Indian art.*

Clark's Gallery and Studio
405 Sosaya Lane
Santa Fe, NM 87501
505-983-8620
*Wood block art by the late Willard Clark.
His grandson, Kevin Ryan, continues the
tradition.*

Conlon Siegal Galleries
135 W. Palace Avenue, Suite 101
Santa Fe, NM 87501
505-820-3300
Ancient textiles and objects.

Cristof's
420 Old Santa Fe Trail
Santa Fe, NM 87501
505-988-9881
Navajo weavings.

Davis Mather Folk Art Gallery
141 Lincoln Avenue
Santa Fe, NM 87501
505-983-1660
*Folk art gallery featuring New Mexican
animal woodcarvings, Mexican folk art,
nontraditional Native American art, and
unpredictable art.*

Dewey Galleries Ltd.
53 Old Santa Fe Trail
Santa Fe, NM 87501
505-982-8632
*Native American art, including watercolor
and sculpture; lithographs by Alan Houser.*

Economos Works of Art
500 Canyon Road
Santa Fe, NM 87501
505-982-6347
*Specializing in fine antiques, pre-
Columbian art, Spanish colonial, silver,
and decorative arts.*

Good Hands Gallery
700 Paseo de Peralta
Santa Fe, NM 87501
505-982-3352
*Hispanic art, both traditional and
contemporary, including bultos and
retablos.*

Kania-Ferrin Gallery
662 Canyon Road
Santa Fe, NM 87501
505-982-8767
*American Indian, Oceanic, and Spanish
colonial art and antiques. Specializing in
basketry.*

Laurel Seth Gallery
112 Paseo de Peralta
Santa Fe, NM 87501
505-988-7349
*A second-generation gallery specializing in
emerging artists.*

LewAllen Contemporary Art
129 W. Palace Avenue
Santa Fe, NM 87501
505-988-8997
*Contemporary art gallery representing
national artists.*

Linda Durham Contemporary Art
12 La Vega
Galisteo, NM 87540
505-466-6600
*Contemporary works by New Mexico
artists.*

Morning Star Gallery
513 Canyon Road
Santa Fe, NM 87501
505-982-8187
*Masterpieces of antique American
Indian art.*

The Munson Gallery
225 Canyon Road
Santa Fe, NM 87501
505-983-1657
*Contemporary art by established and
emerging American artists.*

Nedra Matteucci Fine Art
555 Canyon Road
Santa Fe, NM 87501
505-983-2731
*Traditional representational American and
European artists.*

Niman Fine Art
125 Lincoln Avenue, Suite 116
Santa Fe, NM 87501
505-988-5091
*Contemporary painting and sculpture by
Dan Namingha.*

Owings Dewey Fine Art
76 E. San Francisco Street
Santa Fe, NM 87501
505-982-6244
*Nineteenth- and twentieth-century
American art, painting, drawing, and
sculpture.*

Pachamama
223 Canyon Road
Santa Fe, NM 87501
505-983-4020
*Spanish colonial antiques and Latin
American folk art.*

Peyton Wright
237 E. Palace Avenue
Santa Fe, NM 87501
505-989-9888
Contemporary, ethnographic, Spanish colonial art and antiquities.

Rainbow Man
107 E. Palace Avenue
Santa Fe, NM 87501
505-982-8706
Original photographs by Edward S. Curtis, Native American early textiles and antiques, pawn jewelry, and Mexican collectibles.

Ron Messick Fine Arts
600 Canyon Road
Santa Fe, NM 87501
505-983-9533
Antiques from the Americas.

Scheinbaum & Russek Photography
369 Montezuma, Suite 345
Santa Fe, NM 87501
505-988-5116
Contemporary and vintage twentieth-century photographic prints.

Stephen's Consignment Gallery
2701 Cerrillos Road
Santa Fe, NM 87501
505-471-0802
Traditional and contemporary art purchased or consigned.

Thirteen Moons Gallery
652 Canyon Road
Santa Fe, NM 87501
505-995-8513
The only U.S. gallery devoted exclusively to the art quilt.

Wadle Galleries
128 W. Palace Avenue
Santa Fe, NM 87501
505-983-9219
Representational paintings and sculptures. Native American and Hispanic arts.

Wyeth Hurd Gallery
301 E. Palace Avenue
Santa Fe, NM 87501
505-989-8380
Paintings, drawings, and prints by four generations of the Wyeth-Hurd family.

Zaplin-Lambert Gallery
651 Canyon Road
Santa Fe, NM 87501
505-982-6100
Specializing in works by the early artists of Santa Fe, Taos, and the West.

FURNITURE & RUGS

American Country Collection
620 Cerrillos Road
Santa Fe, NM 87501
505-984-0955
Unique collection of European antique furniture, upholstery, and beds.

Collaborations
544 S. Guadalupe Street
Santa Fe, NM 87501
505-984-3045
A showroom for Ernest Thompson, Sombraje Shutters, and Quimera Galleries.

Crownpoint Navajo Rug Auction
Crownpoint Elementary School
Crownpoint, NM 87313
505-786-5323
An artist's association offering a wide selection of Navajo rugs at auction.

Elements
314 S. Guadalupe Street
Santa Fe, NM 87501
505-982-0055
Largest U.S. importer of sixteenth- to nineteenth-century country antiques from Spain; exclusive U.S. importer of Telar upholstery fabrics from Barcelona.

Foreign Traders
202 Galisteo Street
Santa Fe, NM 87501
505-983-6441
Imported, handcrafted furniture and accessories.

Galisteo Home Furnishings
132 E. Marcy Street
Santa Fe, NM 87501
505-992-3300
Furniture, antiques, lighting, and accessories.

Joelle of Santa Fe, Inc.
Tesuque Flea Market
505-983-5848
Rugs, textiles, and architectural antiques.

Packards West
125 E. San Francisco Street
Santa Fe, NM 87501
505-986-6089
One of the world's leading collections of Oriental carpets from Tibet, Iran, Egypt, Nepal, Romania, Turkey, and Central Asia.

Santa Fe Country Furniture
1708 Cerrillos Road
Santa Fe, NM 87501
505-984-1478
Complete lines of handcrafted, quality Southwest furniture. Rustic leather chairs and recliners.

Santa Fe Oriental Rugs
212 Galisteo Street
Santa Fe, NM 87501
505-982-5152
Old and new Oriental rugs. Repair, cleaning, and appraisals.

Santa Kilim
401 S. Guadalupe Street
Santa Fe, NM 87501
505-988-5122
Oriental rugs of all shapes and sizes.

Seret & Sons
224 Galisteo Street
Santa Fe, NM 87501
505-988-9151
Tribal rugs, custom furniture, and handcarved antique doors.

Southwest Spanish Craftsmen
328 Guadalupe Street
Santa Fe, NM 87501
505-982-1767
Over seventy years of building custom designed furniture.

HOME COMFORTS

BOOKS

Books & More Books
1341 Cerrillos Road
Santa Fe, NM 87501
505-983-5438
New and used art books, Southwest and Native American books, and literature.

Collected Works Bookstore
208-B W. San Francisco Street
Santa Fe, NM 87501
505-988-4226
Santa Fe's booksource since 1978. Fiction, art, Southwest and Native American.

Dumont Maps & Books of the West
314 Mackenzie Street
Santa Fe, NM 87501
505-988-1076
Out-of-print, rare, and limited-edition books. Specializing in the American West.

Garcia Street Books
376 Garcia Street
Santa Fe, NM 87501
505-986-0151
Quality books on art, architecture, and style.

La Fonda Newsstand
La Fonda Hotel
100 E. San Francisco Street
Santa Fe, NM 87501
505-988-1404
Specializing in books of the Southwest;
newspapers and souvenirs.

Margolis & Moss
505-982-1028
By appointment.
Rare and fine books, nineteenth-century
photographs, antiquarian prints, maps, and
old paper ephemera.

Nicholas Potter Bookseller
211 E. Palace Avenue
Santa Fe, NM 87501
Used and rare hardbacks bought and sold.

FOOD

The Chile Shop
109 E. Water Street
Santa Fe, NM 87501
505-983-6080
Variety of ground chile powders, blue
cornmeal and ristras, as well as all things
chile.

Cookworks
316, 318, and 322 S. Guadalupe
  Street
Santa Fe, NM 87501
505-988-7676
Three shops in separate buildings.
Dinnerware and accessories, gourmet
foods, teas and coffee, and kitchen
equipment.

Coyote Cafe General Store
132 W. Water Street
Santa Fe, NM 87501
505-982-2454
Chile products and more from the famous
  restaurant.

El Merendero Posa's
1248 Siler Road
Santa Fe, NM 87505
505-471-4766
Wholesale and retail tamales.

Farmers' Market
505-983-4010
Guadalupe Street near the train
  depot in Santa Fe.
May–November: Tuesday and
  Saturday, 7:00 A.M.–noon.
Fresh produce, green chiles, and other goods
from area vendors.

Gift N' Gourmet
55 Old Santa Fe Trail
Santa Fe, NM 87501
505-982-5953
Chile products and Southwest-designed
tableware.

Ohori's
507 Old Santa Fe Trail
Santa Fe, NM 87501
505-988-7026
Coffee beans, fine teas, chocolates, and
accessories.

Roasted Chile
In the fall, the wonderful smells of roasting
chiles will lead you to "roasters" located in
many supermarket parking lots.

Santa Fe School of Cooking
Plaza Mercado
116 W. San Francisco Street
Santa Fe, NM 87501
505-983-4511
Learn to prepare wonderful Mexican and
Southwestern cuisine.

Señor Murphy Candymaker
La Fonda Hotel
100 E. San Francisco Street
Santa Fe, NM 87501
505-982-0461
Piñon candies, chocolates, chile jellies,
fudges; brittle made in Santa Fe; shipping
available.

Wine and Chile Fiesta
505-438-8060
An international event with tastings,
gourmet dinners, tours, demonstrations,
and seminars with famous winemakers and
chefs.

PLANTS AND POTS

Agua Fria Nursery
1409 Agua Fria
Santa Fe, NM 87505-0907
505-983-4831
Southwestern trees and shrubs, native
plants, roses, bedding plants, houseplants,
and garden supplies.

Jackalope
2820 Cerrillos Road
Santa Fe, NM 87507
505-471-8539
Native plants, houseplants, cacti, and pots
of many shapes and sizes.

Newman's
7501 Cerrillos Road
Santa Fe, NM 87505
505-471-8642
Large selection of native trees, perennials,
roses, and amendments.

Payne's Nurseries and
  Greenhouses
715 St. Michaels Drive
Santa Fe, NM 87501
505-471-8499
Great selection of houseplants, xeric plants,
groundcovers, and perennials.

Plants of the Southwest
Rt. 6 Box 11A
Agua Fria Road
Santa Fe, NM 87501
505-438-8888
Wildflowers, drought-tolerant grasses, and
traditional vegetables.

Santa Fe Greenhouses
2904 Rufina Street
Santa Fe, NM 87505
505-473-2700
Native drought-resistant plants, organic
fertilizer, and pest control.

HOME PRESERVATION
ORGANIZATIONS

Cornerstones Community
  Partnership
P.O. Box 2341
Santa Fe, NM 87501
505-982-9521
A hands-on organization preserving adobe
churches and historical buildings.

Historic Preservation Division,
  Office of Cultural Affairs
228 E. Palace Avenue
Santa Fe, NM 87501
505-827-6320
Administers the State Cultural Properties
Act and the National Historic
Preservation Act.

Historic Santa Fe Foundation
545 Canyon Road
Santa Fe, NM 87501
505-983-2567
Acquires and administers historic proper-
ties, conducts research in order to deter-
mine buildings worthy of preservation, and
maintains historic landmarks and struc-
tures.

Indian Market
505-983-5220
The largest annual juried Native American
market in North America. Third week in
August, on the Santa Fe Plaza.

New Mexico Heritage
  Preservation Alliance
P.O. Box 2490
Santa Fe, NM 87504
505-989-7745
The mission of this alliance is to protect
and preserve the historical resources in
New Mexico.

Santa Fe Historic Design Review Board
City of Santa Fe, Planning Department
200 Lincoln Avenue
Santa Fe, NM 87501
505-955-6605
Reviews the architectural plans of all proposed building and remodeling in the designated historic districts in the city of Santa Fe.

Spanish Colonial Arts Society
750 Camino Lejo
Santa Fe, NM 87501
505-983-4038
Sponsors of the Spanish Market on the Plaza, held the last weekend in July. Also sponsors of the Winter Spanish Market held the first weekend in December. Both are held at the Sweeney Convention Center.

II. THE FACES BEHIND THE PLACES
A listing of those homeowners, businesses, and individuals whose work is represented in this book.

ARCHITECTS, DESIGNERS, AND HOMEBUILDERS

Suby Bowden and Associates
333 Montezuma, Suite 200
Santa Fe, NM 87501
505-983-3755
Architectural planning and industrial design.

Cultural Revival
Jody Apple
HCR 64 Box 18
Chimayo, NM 87522
Importer of Southwestern style, one-of-a-kind pieces of furniture from Java and textiles from India.

Susan Dupepe Interior Design, Inc.
220 McKenzie Street
Santa Fe, NM 87501
505-982-4536
Internationally known residential and commercial designer.

Kitchens by Jeanne
631 Old Santa Fe Trail #1
Santa Fe, NM 87501
505-988-4594
A kitchen design team.

Michael Mahaffy Architects
131 Pedregal Place
Santa Fe, NM 87501
505-984-1232
Listed among Architectural Digest's top one hundred architects.

Ashley Margetson
1012 Calle Lento
Santa Fe, NM 87501
505-988-2221
One-of-a-kind interiors, incorporating antiques, folk art, and other elements.

McDowell Construction
433 W. San Francisco Street
Santa Fe, NM 87501
505-982-5238
Custom home-building since 1976.

Clare Rhoades
10 C Soleado Lane
Santa Fe, NM 87501
505-988-3203
Eclectic, Old World folk art and antiques.

Steven Robinson Architects
322 Read Street
Santa Fe, NM 87501
505-989-8335
A full-service architectural firm, including planning and design.

Jake Rodriguez Architects
466 W. San Francisco Street
Santa Fe, NM 87501
505-983-5497
A full-service architectural firm.

S. Lyn Rose, Ltd.
Susan L. Rose
10645 N. Tatum Boulevard, Suite 200
Phoenix, AZ 85028
480-607-3500
Interior designer. By appointment only.

Jane Smith Interiors
552 Canyon Road
Santa Fe, NM 87501
505-988-4775
Antiques, fabrics, furnishings, and old wood pieces.

Wiseman & Gale & Duncan
150 St. Francis Drive
Santa Fe, NM 87501
505-984-8544
Design, antiques, fine furnishings, and accessories.

Woods Architects-Builders, Inc.
302 Catron Street
Santa Fe, NM 87501
505-988-2413
Coauthor Sharon Woods has led this firm in designing, building, and remodeling Santa Fe's custom homes for more than twenty-five years.

CRAFTSMEN, ARTISTS, PHOTOGRAPHERS, AND WRITERS

Doug Atwill
604 Canyon Road
Santa Fe, NM 87501
505-983-2852
Painter of landscapes.

David Bradley
P.O. Box 5692
Santa Fe, NM 87502
505-471-3791
Contemporary Native American artist; internationally exhibited painter and sculptor.

Joan Brooks Baker
551 Cordova Road, #442
Santa Fe, NM 87501
Fine arts photographer.

Sally Chandler
Works available at:

Parchman Stremmel Galleries
203 N. Presa
San Antonio, TX 78205
210-222-2465

and

Anne Reed Gallery
391 First Avenue North
Ketchum, ID 83340
208-726-3036
Mixed media painter.

Jim Davila
Rt. 5 Box 296 AA
Santa Fe, NM 87501
505-455-2962
Folk artist.

Christine Mather
141 Lincoln Avenue
Santa Fe, NM 87501
505-988-1218
Coauthor of this book, and author of other design and regional art publications, Mather is a freelance writer, art historian, and curator. She also acts as a consultant for the acquisition of regional art.

Carmella Padilla
P.O. Box 2022
Santa Fe, NM 87505
505-471-8821
Cultural writer.

Jack Parsons Photography
P.O. Box 548
Santa Fe, NM 87504
505-474-4704
Documentary, editorial, stock, and architectural photography, with an emphasis on the Southwest.

Schenck Southwest
505-424-6838
Southwest contemporary paintings; original furniture design concepts in the Molesworth tradition.

Southwestern Light
Rebecca Parsons
P.O. Box 548
Santa Fe, NM 87504
505-473-1077
The original Santa Fe–style hand-thrown pottery light fixtures.

Luis Tapia
49-A Las Golondrinas Road
Santa Fe, NM 87505
505-471-3164
Fine and folk art sculptor.

Jerry West
48 Shenandoah Trail
Santa Fe, NM 87505
505-424-3959
Specializing in fireplaces, nichos, and murals.

William Field Design
P.O. Box 1843
Santa Fe, NM 87501
505-988-8888 voice
505-988-7555 fax
Graphic exhibit and design.

GALLERIES, SHOPS, ETC.

Antique Warehouse
530 S. Guadalupe Street
Santa Fe, NM 87501
505-984-1159
Mexican doors, ranch furniture, and Spanish colonial antiques.

Art Culinaire
Stan Barrett
17721 132nd Avenue
Woodinville, WA 98072-8753
800-570-2433
U.S. supplier of French Lacanche ranges made for those who like stoves that are artful as well as practical.

Claiborne Galleries
Located at:

608 Canyon Road
Santa Fe, NM 87501
505-982-8019

and

The Design Center
418 Cerrillos Road
Santa Fe, NM 87501
505-982-5622
Old and new furniture and accessories from around the world.

The Clay Angel
125 Lincoln Avenue
Santa Fe, NM 87501
505-988-4800
Largest collection of traditional ceramics in the United States.

Davis Mather Folk Art Gallery
141 Lincoln Avenue
Santa Fe, NM 87501
505-983-1660
Folk art of the region and beyond. Coauthor Christine Mather is part of this folk art gallery.

Doodlet's
120 Don Gaspar Avenue
Santa Fe, NM 87501
505-983-3771
A shop of whimsical and unique gifts from around the region and world that reflect the offbeat vision and humor of the owner, Theo Raven.

El Rancho de Nambé
Alan France
Plaza el Jardin
17720 North Highway 84/285
Santa Fe, NM 87506
505-455-7922
More than 10,000 square feet of furnishings and antiques on over one acre, including a garden section.

The Flower Market
Guadalupe Street at Manhattan
    Street
Santa Fe, NM 87501
505-982-9663
Many varieties of cut flowers from around the world.

Linda Durham Contemporary Art
12 La Vega
Galisteo, NM 87540
505-466-6600
A twenty-four-year-old gallery representing young, mid-career, and cutting edge artists working in all media. Exhibitions in Galisteo as well as across the country and abroad.

Los Poblanos Inn
4803 Rio Grande Boulevard NW
Los Ranchos de Albuquerque, NM
    87107
505-344-9297
Historic inn set on twenty-five acres in Albuquerque's North Valley.

Mitchell Brown Fine Art, Inc.
8 Tetilla Road
Santa Fe, NM 87505
505-466-1530
Private art dealer of fine American paintings of the West from 1880 through 1950.

Munson Graphics
2754 Agua Fria, Unit E
Santa Fe, NM 87505
505-424-4112
Fine art publishers developing prints and cards for fine art collections.

Nedra Matteucci Galleries
1075 Paseo De Peralta
Santa Fe, NM 87501
505-982-4631
Specializing in American art, especially the Taos Society of Artists.

Pennysmith's
4022 Rio Grande Boulevard NE
Albuquerque, NM 87101
505-345-2353
Custom invitations and party accessories.

Posters of Santa Fe
111 E. Palace Avenue
Santa Fe, NM 87501
505-982-6645
Finest selection of posters and notecards in the Southwest.

Rancho Manzana
Jody Apple
HCR 64 Box 18
Chimayo, NM 87522
505-351-2227
Beautiful lavender fields and gardens in an authentic northern New Mexico historic setting.

Susan's Christmas Shop
115 E. Palace Avenue
Santa Fe, NM 87501
505-983-2127
Traditional and Southwest Christmas ornaments and decorated Easter eggs; open all year long.

INDEX

acequia, 233
adobe homes, 11, 28, 36–57
air, 199, 199–240
Arroyo Hondo, 111
art
    folk, 174, 179, 192–97
    garden, 22–25
    Native American, 59, 61, 62
    regional, 36–38, 96, 119, 174
    See also religious art
Atwill, Doug, 226–31, 233

bancos, 122–23, 199
baths, 152–57, 164, 179
beams, 22, 26, 28–31, 72, 107
bedrooms, 56, 118, 129, 146–51, 158, 179
Biggerstaff, Alice Ann, 191
blue, 144
books/built-ins, 48–51
Busch, Joy and Bernie, 233–35

Canyon Road, 11, 56–57
ceilings, 28–31
ceramics. *See* pottery
Chandler, Sally, 168
collections, 48, 50, 53–54, 60, 61, 92, 176–77, 195–97
colors, 67–71, 144, 191–94
corbels, 22, 28–31, 107
courtyards, 206, 209
cupboards, 188–89, 238

dados, 88, 238
devotional art. *See* religious art

dining areas, 56, 60, 94–97, 101, 104, 112, 135
    outside, 206–9, 230
Doodlet's, 172–79
doors, 16–19, 46, 105, 144

earth, 12–65
El Molinito, 74
entryways, 11, 20–21, 44, 59, 102, 107, 144, 237

fall, 69
fire, 67–139
fireplaces, 37, 59, 60, 64, 72–79, 101, 107, 114, 121, 131, 179, 214
firewood, 78
flowers, 68, 142–43, 201, 214–25
folk art, 174, 179, 192–97
fountains, 164, 166–71

garden art, 222–25
garden gates, 210–13
garden pots, 220–21
gardens, 173, 202–13, 220–26
    ramadas, 241

hardware, 124
Higgins, Victor, 37, 38

Jackson, John Brinckerhoff, 36
Jones, Anita Romero, 104

kitchens, 45, 53, 60, 80–87, 179

La Luz pottery, 163
lintels, 30
living rooms. *See salas*
Los Poblanos y La Quinta, 160–65

Matteucci, Nedra and Richard, 58
Meem, John Gaw, 76, 160, 163
metalwork, 124, 160
Molesworth, Thomas, 37, 38
murals, 88

Native American art, 59, 61, 62
nichos, 41, 67, 90, 99, 101, 107, 114, 132

O'Keeffe, Georgia, 64
outdoor rooms, 204–5

Padilla, Carmella, 129
painted walls, 88–93
passageways, 20–21, 99, 232–33
pools, 141, 166–67
portals, 53, 162, 173, 216–19, 230, 238
pottery, 37, 38, 44, 61, 62, 102, 108–9, 163, 220–21

quiet corners, 158–59

ramadas, 240
religious art, 53–54, 61, 67, 90, 101–9, 116, 129, 133–39, 176–77, 191

Rose, S. Lyn, 42, 43

salas, 22–27, 99, 174, 183, 229
Sangre de Cristo Mountains, 7, 14, 67, 68, 199, 201
Schenck, Bill, 36, 37, 38
shelves, 48–51, 92
skulls, 64–65
spring, 143
stencils, 92
straw-bale houses, 110–15
summer, 199, 202

Tapia, Luis, 129, 131, 132
Tapia, Sergio, 132
Tesuque, 182–85
tiles, 152, 156–57, 160, 164, 179
tinwork, 180–81
    lighting fixtures, 126–27
trasteros, 188–89, 238

Vierra, Carlos, 76
village farmhouse, 236–38

wall paintings, 88–93
water, 140–97
windows, 11, 186–87
winter, 14
woodworking, 32–35

ABOUT THE AUTHORS
AND PHOTOGRAPHER

Christine Mather, a recognized authority on Spanish colonial art, has worked as a museum curator and helped found and run the Davis Mather Folk Art Gallery. The author of *Santa Fe Style*, *True West*, *Native America*, and *Santa Fe Christmas*, she has lectured throughout the United States on art and cultural history.

Sharon Woods, the owner of Woods Architects-Builders, Inc., has built and renovated many Santa Fe homes. The coauthor, with Mather, of *Santa Fe Style*, she has been an active force in preservation and building in Santa Fe.

Jack Parsons, Mather's longtime collaborator, has worked to document the Southwest in both film and photography for more than twenty-five years. His photographs appear in countless publications.